MIND
BODY
HOME

TRANSFORM YOUR LIFE
ONE ROOM AT A TIME

TISHA MORRIS

Mind Body Home: Transform Your Life One Room at a Time © 2020 Tisha Morris

All rights reserved. No part of this book may be used or reproduced in any manner whatsoever, including internet usage, without written permission from Tisha Morris, except in the case of brief quotations embodied in critical articles and reviews.

Book formatting by Amit Dey | amitdey2528@gmail.com

First Edition, 2013
Llewellyn Publications
ISBN: 9780738736945

Second Edition, 2018
Tisha Morris
ISBN: 9781718178915

Third Edition, 2020
Tisha Morris
ISBN: 9781734770605

OTHER BOOKS BY THIS AUTHOR

Clutter Intervention: How Your Stuff is Keeping You Stuck
(Llewellyn Worldwide 2018)

Decorating With the Five Elements of Feng Shui
(Llewellyn Worldwide 2015)

Feng Shui Your Life: The Quick Guide to Decluttering Your Home and Renewing Your Life (Turner Publishing 2010), reprint of *27 Things to Feng Shui Your Home*

TABLE OF CONTENTS

PREFACE xi

INTRODUCTION xiii

- My Life as a House xiv
- The Mind Body Home Connection xvii
- Relating Mind-Body Principles xix
- Our Home as a Mirror xx

PART I: GETTING TO KNOW YOUR HOME xxiii

CHAPTER 1: Your Home's Origin - Location 1

- What is Energy? 2
- Detecting the Earth's Energy 3
- Neighborhoods 4
- Selecting a Home Site 8
- T-Intersections, Dead Ends, and Cul-de-Sacs 9
- Using Intuition 10

CHAPTER 2: Your Home's Personality - Numerology 13

- Numbers as Archetypes 14
- Numerology for Homes 14

CHAPTER 3: Your Home's Body - The Shape of the House
           and How it Shapes You 25
- Childhood Home 27
- Too Little, Too Big, or Just Right? 27
- Grounding In 30
- What Architectural Style is Best for You? 31
- Old Home or New Home 36

CHAPTER 4: Your Home's Path - Floor Plan of the House 39
- Flow of Energy 40
- Do's and Don'ts for Interior Door Placement 41
- The Bagua Map 41
- Missing Corners 45
- Front Door 46
- Front Entrance 47
- Hallways 50
- Stairways 51
- Bathrooms 52
- Garage 56

CHAPTER 5: Your Home's Past - Previous Owners 59
- Patterns of Energy 61
- Foreclosed Homes 63
- Ghosts and Other Entities 65
- Ghost Busting 67
- But My Ghost is Friendly! 70
- Space Clearing 70
- Steps for Space Clearing 72
- How Often Should You Space Clear? 73

CHAPTER 6: Our Energy, Our Emotions, and Our Stuff. 75
- Energy or Aura Fields 76
- The Chakras. 79
- Inanimate Objects Have Feelings Too 82
- Furniture 83
- Clutter and the Art of Detaching 85
- Objects of Our Expression 88

PART II: YOUR HOME SPEAKS YOUR MIND 91

CHAPTER 7: The Language of the Home. 95

CHAPTER 8: Floors - Levels of Consciousness 101
- Foundation 102
- 'Settling' Into Your Home 103
- Basement 105
- What's Really Down There? 107
- Basements and Boundaries 108
- Basements and Flooding. 109
- Out of Sight, Out of Mind? 110
- Main Level 111
- 2ND Floor 113
- Where Should Your Home Office Be Located? 114
- Attic. 115

CHAPTER 9: Structural Components - The Bones of the Home . 119
- Framework 120
- Flooring. 122
- Ceiling 123
- Roof. 125

- Walls 126
- Fireplace 128
- Stairs 128
- Windows 130
- Doors 131

CHAPTER 10: Rooms: Our Many Parts and Personas 135
- Bathroom 137
- Bedroom 139
- Closet 141
- Den (or Living Room) 142
- Garage 143
- Transitional Spaces 144
- Kitchen 145

CHAPTER 11: Mechanicals: The Functioning Organ Systems .. 147
- Plumbing 148
- Electricity 151
- Internet/Telephone 153
- Heating and Air Systems 154

CHAPTER 12: Outdoor Spaces: How We Relate to Others 157
- Front and Back of Home 158
- Front Porch 161
- Patio/Deck 162
- Balcony 163
- Fence 164
- Garden 165
- Driveway 166

- Swimming Pool 167
- Trees. 168

CHAPTER 13: Encroachments: What We Attract. 171
- Ants 173
- Flies. 173
- Cockroaches. 174
- Mice 174
- Burglar 175
- Ghosts. 177

CONCLUSION: Integrating Your Mind Body and Home 179
- Household Accidents 180
- Repairs and Maintenance 181
- Improvements 183
- Renovation 185
- Renting Your Home. 187
- Moving 188
- Conclusion 190
- Reference of Mind Body Home Connections 191

Bibliography. 199
About the Author 201

PREFACE

This book was first published in 2012 inspired from my experiences with my own homes in conjunction with my work with feng shui clients. Since then, I've moved cross-country, got married, and have lived in eight more spaces I've called home. During these years, I've used this book for my own referencing many times as my subconscious continues to communicate loudly through my homes. I believe more than ever that this book is an invaluable resource in bringing more consciousness into our lives via our immediate environment.

Since the first edition of this book, both of my parents have passed away. Between this loss and so many moves, I've been forced to reconstruct my narrative of what home is. The paradox has been facing the reality that our home is not a physical place. And yet it is the closest we have to externalize this desire for feeling at home while here on Earth. Our physical home can provide a grounding that allows us to connect with our soul. It is an externalized representation of ourselves, which I believe is why we seek home improvement and the desire to come home to a peaceful sanctuary, not to mention the purpose of using feng shui principles.

Even though I've made strides in finding home within myself, my physical home remains my second skin and integral to feeling grounded. Based on new insights and experiences, this book has been updated accordingly through redactions and additions. I hope this book helps you discover more deeply the home within yourself as well as your physical home.

Tisha
March 11, 2020

INTRODUCTION

Eventually everything connects.
—Charles Eames

Throughout our lives, we live in many different spaces - our childhood home, dorm rooms, our first apartment, our first home, and many more spaces in between and along the way. Think back to the times when you moved into a new home. It most likely coincided with a major life change - marriage, divorce, new baby, new job, school, graduation, downsizing, upsizing, or simply starting over. We never forget the homes we've lived in and energetically they never forget us. Our homes are a part of us and we are a part of them.

Soon after you move into your home, your energy and the energy of your home begin to merge. Just like settling into a long-term relationship, you each begin to feed off the other's energy. Your home becomes a projection of you - physically, mentally, and emotionally. These projections start to show up around the house in a variety of ways. The most obvious example is that a messy home symbolizes a messy or scattered mind. But what about a clogged toilet, leaky roof, or a fallen tree? Each aspect of your home correlates with an aspect of your physical, mental, or emotional wellbeing.

Consider the current state of your home. Have you blown a fuse lately? Are there recurring problems with your home that you can never seem to get resolved? Is it in need of a renovation or just minor cosmetic touches?

Do you have a water leak? Do you have problems with a certain type of insect invading your house? Any of these problems and many more are actually projections of what is going on in your life. By simply looking around your home, you can see the current state of your life. And by making changes to your home, you make correlating changes to yourself.

Our home consists of an array of swirling energies that affect us on subtle and profound levels of which most of us are not aware. Imagine for a moment an unseen world of energy in your home. This unseen, nonphysical world is made up of energy emitted from the earth, from the objects in your home, from previous occupants, and most importantly from your energy field. Understanding how the energies in your home affect you and, likewise, how you affect it can profoundly change the way you view your home. Furthermore, changing the way you live in your home can dramatically change your life.

Our home is more than a physical shell. It is the space with which we are most intimately connected. We cry, laugh, dream, make love, expose and express ourselves more in our home than anywhere else. It is the space in which we are the most vulnerable. Second only to our physical body, it is our shell from the rest of the world. It is a container for our thoughts and emotions. Our home is an energetic expression and physical extension of who we are. While other spaces we occupy, such as our car or office, along with public spaces, have a host of influential energies, none are we as connected with as our home[1].

My Life as a House

This interrelationship between our personal energy and that of our home became clear to me in 2006. I veered off my usual dog-walking route and noticed a *For Sale* sign in the yard of the 1930s Hollywood-style, adobe bungalow. Sitting among craftsmen bungalows and Victorians in

---

[1] Throughout the book, I use the terms "home" and "house" with intention each time. *House* refers to the building structure itself. *Home* is more personal and refers to not only the house but also the aliveness it contains as a result of our human energy.

the historic east Nashville neighborhood where I lived, the house had a peculiar and unique charm. The next day I called my real estate agent. Upon walking in, I knew I was home.

However, I was quickly overwhelmed when I got the inspection report back. It needed a complete overhaul. It had never had central air and therefore needed all new duct work. The electrical system was still on a fuse box. And the house was inundated by plumbing problems due to the outdated and brittle PVC pipes. This was not to mention the aesthetic alterations that would be required throughout - from the canary yellow kitchen (including the ceiling) - to every light switch installed upside down. After already making extensive cosmetic repairs over the last five years to my 1920s bungalow, I had been looking forward to a low maintenance house, maybe even a brand new house - not a renovation. That's when a dear friend of mine said, "You either do it all now or gradually over time." She wasn't just talking about the house. She was talking about me - a renovation of myself.

During this time, I was looking to downsize in order to transition out of practicing law into a more fulfilling career. I had just received a fine arts degree in Interior Design, but still couldn't find anything that would satisfy me. In moments of clarity, I knew I had a calling, so to speak, but I couldn't figure out what it was. I read every self-help and career-transitioning book available.

My personal life was about as consistent as my professional life - in and out of relationships with seemingly poor decision-making. After a significant break-up, I knew I needed to make changes. As a typical Cancer sign, I had become completely co-dependent with my home during this tumultuous time. It was my safe haven and a storehouse for all the emotions I had experienced over the previous five years. It was the same reason I knew what I needed to do: sell my home and start over. That's when this charming bungalow showed up in my life also in need of an overhaul and fresh start.

With the reassurance of smooth real estate transactions, I knew it was time to start my next renovation project, except this one would go deeper than anything I'd previously undertaken. For the next year, this house and I underwent simultaneous transformations. As I peeled away the old layers and made upgrades, I discovered that this house, along with myself, was a diamond in the rough that just needed some love.

With each improvement I made, I could see the correlating changes occurring within myself. From upgrading the electrical system to putting in a new HVAC system to simply painting the walls, I noticed how each of these changes affected me - physically, mentally, and emotionally. For example, as the central air was installed, my own breathing was eased through yoga and meditation. As the electrical panel was upgraded from a fuse box to a 200-volt panel, my nervous system calmed and I learned not to be so reactive. I painted each room a different color and, in doing so, a new aspect of myself came to life with each room. As I expanded the renovation to the guesthouse, I tapped into new aspects of myself as a healer.

There was a particularly memorable moment during the time when I owned both homes for a two-week period. I was running on fumes getting the new house in order while moving out of the former house. I was completely exhausted. Within a 30-minute window, the HVAC systems on both homes went down. Both needed the same part - a new fan. The message was that I had exhausted myself, out of breath, and needed to take a break. It was moments such as this that I knew my subconscious mind was speaking to me through my home. I was also having vivid dreams of homes, which provided more information that I luckily didn't have to experience through my home.

By the end of that year, I had fallen in love with this house and myself. The last touches I made on the home were painting the trim around the exterior windows. I had finished making the necessary repairs and upgrades and could now focus on the improvements to allow this home to express its unique charm and beauty for the world to see. As I painted the windows with a turquoise trim characteristic of traditional adobe-style homes, I was expressing my own voice out into the world in a new way.

Just as angels and guides communicate to some people and dreams and visions come to others, homes speak to me. Specifically, this house taught me the subconscious language in which all our homes speak to us. Years later, I came across Carl Jung's autobiography, *Memories, Dreams, Reflections,* where he recounts the powerful symbolism his house held for him as he was building it. This correlation was further explored in *The House of C. G. Jung,* a project spearheaded by Carl Jung's grandson, Andreas Jung.

During my year renovating the house, I tapped into my soul's work. I also purged so much of my past, which opened up a vacuum of space for allowing new opportunities to come in. And did they ever. Within a month of moving in, I started teaching yoga and soon realized that I had a gift for working with subtle energies. After studying and training in various modalities, I started an energy healing and feng shui practice. One year later, I sold the house to purchase a home with my partner of whom I met the exact day I moved into this house that changed my life. That home will forever be a part of me just as all of our homes are forever a part of us.

I experienced first-hand just how interrelated our energy is with our home. I also experienced how important our home is in living consciously. When you make changes to your home, you make changes to yourself. When you make *conscious* changes to your home, you can *transform* your life and uncover your *soul*.

The Mind Body Home Connection

As alternative medicine and holistic living have become mainstream, so many wonderful modalities are offered in almost any community and city. At the same time, our home is an essential part of holistic living and right at our fingertips. Holistic is about bringing the whole into balance. If our home is out of order or balance, then it will be difficult, if not impossible, for our life to be in order. Our living spaces are integral to this balancing equation. Our body is a manifestation of our mind and our home is a further extension of the mind and body. Everything is energy and affects one another. This is the power of the *mind body home* connection.

For thousands of years in all cultures, traditions, and religions, the house has been closely connected to, or used as a metaphor for, the soul. In Christianity, the body is referred to as the *temple of the soul*. In literature, it was Nathaniel Hawthorne's *The House of Seven Gables* that made this connection. And Gaston Bachelard offered a poetic summation of this interrelationship in *The Poetics of Space*. In Hollywood, *Life as a House* depicted the stages of building a house as representative of the characters' lives and relationships. For Jungian dream analysts, along with all prevailing dream interpreters, the house symbolizes the Self and the way we build our lives - with each room and component of the house representing aspects of ourselves.

The connection between a house and our body can even be found in architecture and often referred to as sacred geometry. Historically, the proportions of the body have been used in architecture to determine the basic proportions of spaces. This was the meaning behind Leonardo Da Vinci's well-known illustration, *The Vitruvian Man,* used by architect Vitruvius himself in designing spaces.

The connection between spaces and how they affect humans is widely known as *feng shui*. Originating in China and now used worldwide, feng shui is a science that relates how the energy in spaces affects the mind and body of its inhabitants. Feng shui is a science that falls under the umbrella of Chinese medicine, along with acupuncture and Qigong, to name a few. It's not coincidental that Chinese medicine integrates the mind, the body, and the home as integral components for a balanced and happy life.

The Hindu version of feng shui, called *vastu shastra* or simply *vastu*, may have been the first living science to make the *mind body home* connection. The Vedas, written in approximately 2500 B.C, is a treatise on Ayurvedic medicine, Yoga, and Vastu. In Vastu, the body is renowned as a living example of perfect architecture. Just like Chinese Medicine, the basis of health and wellbeing in Indian culture is comprised of bringing balance to the mind, body, and home. While Western medicine has historically only focused on treating the physical body post-disease, Eastern medicine focuses on balancing the mind, body, and home for preventive and curative purposes.

As the West and East slowly merge, Western medicine is only beginning to touch on preventive medicine by borrowing from eastern cultures. As such, more and more people are realizing how important their home and environment is on their overall wellbeing. As we awaken to this network of energetic connections of our mind, body, and home, we become more conscious within our own life and begin to open the door to the heart of our own home.

This energetic connection between our Self and our home is a living example of the connections within our Universe. Our home connects us to everything and highlights the universal truth that everything is connected - from our neighbors, to the land we live on, to the plants and animals, and across the globe everywhere. Second only to our physical body, our home is our primary connection to the Earth and is therefore a laboratory for self-exploration, growth, and transformation. With the evolution of the home and the human mind, we are now living in a time when the home is more than just a metaphor, but a reflection or projection of ourselves.

Relating Mind-Body Principles

The relationship that the home has with its owners is very similar to the relationship the body has with its mind. The first breakthrough in the mind-body field was in proving that stress is a major contributor, if not the cause, of some physical ailments and diseases. Research now shows that many physical problems are psychosomatic. When I went to a medical doctor in the 1990's for chronic stomach problems, the doctor asked if I was under any stress. When I told him I was perfectly happy as I was planning my wedding, he questioned whether I should be getting married because of the physical results my body was showing.

At the time, I thought the doctor was not only crazy, but also rude and inappropriate. In hindsight, I should have looked closer as it was not until my divorce when my stomach problems suddenly stopped. At that time, the relationship between the mental and emotional body with the physical body was not widely known and as accepted as it is today. Years later, when I made the connection, it became the inspiration behind my studying and training to become an energy healer.

Now it's nearly impossible to have a conversation about chronic pains and other dis-eases without some questions about stress and emotions. There are now many mind-body books, pioneered by Louise Hay's *Heal Your Body*, that relate each common disease and body part ailment to its mental or emotional root cause. Even Western doctors are prescribing yoga and meditation to their patients to combat many psychosomatic illnesses.

When our subconscious mind cannot reach our conscious mind, it often uses our body through which to send its messages. Pain almost always gets our attention. Repressed emotions, trauma, negative emotional or thought patterns, or anything that is not processed in real time is stored in the body. Ideally, mental or emotional stressors are dealt with and released before reaching the physical body. If not, however, over time the root cause will seek outward manifestation in the form of pain or illness. Pain is information or a 'red flag' that there is something mentally or emotionally out of balance. This information may present itself in our home instead of, or in conjunction with, our physical body.

Our Home as a Mirror

Just as the body is an extension or manifestation of the mind, the home is as well. In the physical world, we take up residence in our physical body with our home being the next layer. The home is in essence our second layer of skin. Although no two bodies or homes are the same, both take on a rather typical structure: a framework and skeleton; windows and eyes; nervous system and electricity; central air and breath; and so on.

On a subconscious level, we have formed houses to fit the same mold as our own physical structure. Just as a computer was built to replicate the human brain, our homes are built to replicate our energy. Birds build their nests to form the curvature of their bodies. We have built homes to not only fit, but mirror ourselves. We take comfort in a space that matches us physically and energetically.

While homes started out as a cave, or roof for shelter from the elements, they have evolved just as we have evolved. Our homes have become sophisticated beings that match where we are on our journey - be it a dorm room, a mansion, or a cozy bungalow. Just as our soul, or spirit, is housed in the physical body, our mind and body take up space and refuge in the home. While the home is separate or detached from our body, the unseen energy connection is not.

In Part I you will begin to understand the energy of your house before you ever set foot inside. The shape, structure, floor plan, and even street address make up your home's unique fingerprint. The energy of your home begins to shape areas of your life. Simultaneously, your personal energy patterns made up of your thoughts, beliefs, and emotions also take up residence in your home. These energies merge into an energy soup that is unique to you and your home. This starts to manifest throughout your home and into your life.

Part II decodes the most common symbols of the home from the ground up. Each aspect of the house symbolizes some aspect of one's self, including rooms, mechanicals, components, and outdoor areas of the home from the ground up and extending to the exterior of the home. You will be able to access all of this information and bring to light your own subconscious mind. Being more in tune with the energy in your home will allow you to make conscious changes in your life. When you make changes to your home, you make changes to your life.

PART I

GETTING TO KNOW YOUR HOME

*[T]hey are beautiful, ordered, harmonious – yes, all these things.
But especially, and what strikes to the heart, they live.*

— The Timeless Way of Building

Before you ever set foot into your home, there is a reality going on within the walls and under the roof that has little to do with you. Your home has its own distinct path, personality, and future. It has its own soul. A building is made up of walls, windows, doors, cabinets, stairs, and other components that are repeated throughout. The configuration of these components and materials will determine to a large degree the pattern of events that take place within that space.

The soul of a space is conceived when the site has been selected and the blueprints are drawn up in tandem with the intention of the homeowner, builder, and/or architect. In *Places of the Soul*, the author describes the process of how a building is 'ensouled' from the viewpoint of a western architect:

"Soul can incarnate progressively into a building as it progressively gains substance from wish, through idea, planning, constructional design, building and occupation. Each stage develops, deepens, and extends that which had come before. They are stages which alternate from aesthetic to practical but, with these aspects inseparable throughout, are stages of continuous process of incarnation into substance until we architects complete our task, leaving a shell for life which will continue to grow."[2]

Every stage of a house being built plays a role in the creation of the soul of a home. Christopher Day further explains the importance of the energy of the construction workers: "Even before occupants breathe life into a building, even before it is finished, the process of ensouling can be well advanced."[3]

The energy of each stage of the home is crucial starting from the very beginning. The stages in which the home is built are akin to the nine months a baby is forming and growing in the womb. It is said that babies are aware of the energy of the mother and those around it while in the womb. Homes are the same way. If construction workers are energetically mistreating the home in any way, unfortunately that energy is within the home. In the case of one of my clients building her home, she placed signs throughout the home directing the workers where to put their trash and cigarette butts. Being in the construction business, she had witnessed too many homes being constructed where the workers threw their trash in the foundation and simply built over it.

Once homeowners move in, a new stage of the home's life begins. This puts into motion a whole new array of energy that continues to build, homeowner after homeowner. Because of the initial energy of the home, patterns will emerge and repeat over time in the home and in the lives of the occupants. However, before this happens a home forms its own personality. Similar to each person having their own individualized fingerprint or astrological chart, a home embodies its own essence prior to its occupants ever moving in. In fact, an astrological chart of your home can be conducted for the year it was built using western astrology and/or feng shui astrology.

---

[2] Christopher Day, Places of the Soul: Architecture and Environmental Design as a Healing Art (London: The Aquarian Press 1990), 106
[3] Christopher Day, p. 136.

The parcel of land the home is built upon, its property address, its shape and floor plan, along with every occupant who has ever lived there, all have an effect on the energy of a space prior to you ever walking through the door. Like a first date, you are meeting this home and will over time get to know all of the baggage it comes with – for better or for worse. To make the energy soup even more interesting, we then move in our energy, emotions, and furniture with our own baggage.

In Part I you will have an understanding of your home on a whole new level. You will see your home for what it is, how it can best support you, and ways in which it could bring up challenges for you and your family as well. We always end up in the space that is a vibrational match to us. That being said, the process of finding your 'soul home' can be easier if you have the knowledge and awareness to know what's the best fit for you. In doing so, your home will be a supportive environment that will bring you an abundance of health, wealth, and happiness.

Part I looks at your home from a macro perspective first starting with the location in Chapter 1. The spot of Earth that is chosen as the building site is the first energetic consideration that will determine the destiny of the space and its occupants. From there, Chapters 2-5 will take a closer look at the individual characteristics of your home. Finally, Chapter 6 will explore what happens when your energy moves in, along with your furniture and personal items.

CHAPTER 1

YOUR HOME'S ORIGIN - LOCATION

I would give a thousand furlongs of sea for an acre of barren ground.

—Shakespeare

Location, Location, Location. This is one principle that feng shui practitioners and realtors, will always agree upon. It's common knowledge in the real estate market that the Number 1 rule is location. You can change just about anything about a house, but not its location. It's not coincidental that feng shui was founded upon this same principle.

Feng shui was originally used for the purpose of locating the best burial sites for Chinese royalty. Feng shui practitioners were originally considered 'doctors' accessible only to the Imperial Palace and were held to secrecy punishable by death. Feng shui secrets slowly made their way to the people and were later used to locating the best sites for living spaces. Four thousand years later, these principles still apply, even in our man-made world of subdivisions and lofts. Historically, feng shui has predominantly been the practice of locating auspicious places and spaces. It was actually much later that feng shui moved inside the home and used for the interior of spaces.

The word *feng shui* translates to *wind water*. *Feng*, or wind, represents chi or energy, while Shui, or water, refers to fortune. In essence, feng shui means being in alignment with the energy of fortune. Fortune not only applies to financial abundance, but also to health, relationships, family, and overall happiness. It is for these rewards that the art and science of feng shui has continued to be practiced worldwide.

Almost everyone has experienced the feng shui of a space without even realizing it. Have you ever moved into a space and immediately bad things started happening - job loss, divorce, illness, or a combination. Or perhaps you were in alignment with the energy of fortune and were blessed with good things - a pregnancy, job promotion, or meeting your soul mate. Even if your experience wasn't as dramatic, you can look back on your homes and see a pattern while living in different spaces. While we can't completely blame our home for bad things happening, often the timing of events cannot be overlooked.

What is Energy?

Energy is the all-pervading universal life force that flows through all that is. When it comes to describing energy in spaces, the word *chi* is often used because of its origin in feng shui and Chinese Medicine. There is ultimately only one source of energy that has been given many names, such as God, Universal Energy, Source, Divine Love, Universal Love, among others. Like a crystal prism, this energy flows and refracts through everything - galaxies, Earth, humans, food, plants, electronics, and even a manufactured vinyl chair from the 1970s. The Sun is our primary source of energy in the Milky Way galaxy and has even been considered a God, or deity, in its own right. Even that which we consider *our* Sun is an offshoot of universal energy, sometimes referred to as the Central Sun.

From a scientific perspective, chi, or energy, is electromagnetic energy. Electromagnetic energy waves are emitted from the core of the Earth, through the layers, up to the surface, and into our atmosphere. This energy is actually a byproduct of the Sun. Planet Earth receives the Sun's energy, keeping what it needs to maintain its equilibrium and reflecting back that which it doesn't need via the atmosphere. We humans are the beneficiaries of this amazing process.

Since Earth acts as our host through gravity, she is our benefactor of energy from the sun. It is this strong magnetic pull through electromagnetic energy that keeps us grounded, literally and energetically, to Planet Earth. Earth maintains the thermostat so that we can exist and live under habitable conditions. When thought of in these terms it seems absurd that we would want to live any other way than in harmony with Mother Earth, let alone jeopardize Earth's built-in HVAC system. If this sounds like a lot of science, it is and that's the point. Energy is not *woo-woo*, it's electromagnetic energy that allows us to be here.

Detecting the Earth's Energy

The Earth's terrain, directions, earth elements, and colors are all visible expressions of the Earth's energy. There are also invisible lines of energy below the Earth's surface that affect life on Earth. Consequently, some areas are more auspicious and prosperous than others. The Earth's energy below the surface is often expressed on the surface through its topography. This is the essence of feng shui and other environmental sciences that have been studied and passed down for centuries.

One of the primary methods of studying the Earth's energy below the visible surface is *geomancy*. It resulted from a translation of feng shui in the 19th Century by Christian missionaries in China and is still practiced, primarily in Europe. Geomancy is a method of divination used to interpret the visible topography and invisible ley lines of the land. Many sacred sites are located on auspicious lines that lie below the Earth's surface detected and made known by geomancy. It is theorized that Stonehenge, among other sacred sites, lay along powerful ley lines connecting a powerful underground energy grid.

A great importance was placed on locating sites for churches, temples, and mosques. For example, geomancy was used to locate power spots.

Christian cathedrals were often sited on old pagan sites because they were considered power spots. Priests would also use geomancy to locate sites and harness the power of the sites. The direction was also an important consideration with Eastern-facing being the preferential siting of most temples and churches.

You can start your own geomancy practice with the use of dowsing rods. Dowsing rods are copper wires still used by farmers to locate underground waterlines for digging wells. They can also be used to detect underground waterways, ley lines. energy vortices or other energetic disturbances in and around the land.

While these deliberate location techniques are not commonly practiced today, the importance of location cannot be underestimated. Living and functioning in an environment with positive energy, or chi, emanating from the Earth will have a profound effect on one's health, wellbeing, and overall prosperity. There is a reason why feng shui has been highly revered for thousands of years and continues to be practiced with steadfast results. Entire cultures, such as Native Americans, Celtic Shamans, and Aborigines, have lived in harmony with the Earth simply as a way of life. Their respect and intuition of the land should serve as a model for living in harmony with Mother Earth.

Neighborhoods

The first step in selecting a home is realizing that not every spot of land on Earth is meant for inhabiting. This is clearly the case with harsh conditions in certain deserts and mountaintops, but it's also the case within certain lots in suburbs and neighborhoods. Just because a builder puts a house on a lot, doesn't mean it's suitable for living or that it will be a supportive environment for a prosperous and happy life. Yes, you might be able to survive, but will you be able to thrive?

For most of us, our home site selection usually starts with deciding what neighborhood we want to live in. Again, *location, location, location* is the mantra in not only selecting a home, but a neighborhood too. This was a hard lesson I learned a few years ago. I was wooed by a gorgeous new-construction home. It was on the very edge of a great neighborhood. But what a difference a few streets can make. Because of its less-than-desirable location, we were able to afford it. We thought the beauty of the house would be enough to override the neighborhood. Unfortunately, we were wrong.

For the first year, we enjoyed our beautiful new home. As we entered the second year, the modern aesthetics started to wear off as the undesirable qualities of the neighborhood became more apparent. Although it was a seemingly quiet, residential street, it had lots of traffic due to being on the bus line. The street was long and straight with no breaks, which allowed cars to speed up and down the street. I witnessed several animals being hit by cars, which was heartbreaking.

Running along the back of the house was a train track and a less than desirable street beyond there. Due to its accessibility, the street experienced a high-rate of break-ins. Needless to say, the street had bad feng shui. In fact, it had everything you should avoid in selecting a neighborhood, which is why I am sharing this story. When we realized we couldn't take it any longer we put our home on the market. My partner and I joked that we needed a neighborhood stager rather than a home stager.

Here are some things to consider when choosing a neighborhood:

Route in and out- As you drive the route in and out of your neighborhood or potential neighborhood, notice what types of homes, businesses, and services you pass. Avoid homes or streets where you have to pass a large cemetery, junkyard, cellphone tower, or a service business that is inherently toxic. Also avoid living in spaces with a view of such sites. Do you pass by uplifting homes, businesses, or parks or do you pass by abandoned buildings, suffering businesses, or any sites that seem oppressive to you?

In my previous home, the quickest way in and out of the neighborhood meant that I had to pass through a run-down part of town in order to quickly get to the interstate. The longer route took me through a more desirable area, but there was a particular hairpin intersection that I always dreaded and was the site of many accidents. Either route was unpleasant and depleted my energy.

Our subconscious mind is constantly picking up on our environment and taking notes. If you pass a cemetery every day to and from work, it will bring your energy down whether you are aware of it or not. Compare this with passing through a beautiful and abundant park-like setting or thriving businesses. Not only does your visual surrounding affect your mood, but your overall energy as well.

Rhythm of a Block- Have you ever lived in a house or multi-story unit with a great view until a new structure was built next door or across from you? Suddenly the whole feel of your home is changed. In urban neighborhoods, it is common for cheaper homes that are either dilapidated or in disrepair to be torn down and replaced by newer and bigger homes. This is referred to as *infill housing*. If there are no building restrictions in the neighborhood, then builders will usually build as large a house as they can fit on the lot, regardless of the size of the other homes on the block. This creates incongruence in the rhythm of the block. The disparity of home sizes also creates inauspicious chi for the smaller homes nearby and the large home as well.

Well-planned subdivisions will have slightly curved streets, sidewalks, and homes that are similar in size with a varying degree of styles and shapes of homes. In subdivisions where all the homes look exactly the same, the block lacks a rhythm. Think of music with one note. In urban areas with mixed-use spaces, be mindful of large buildings nearby. It is best not to live in a building that is dwarfed by another building nearby. This can lead to feelings of inferiority, being blocked or stunted in your endeavors. Likewise, living in a home that towers over others can lead to feelings of superiority or arrogance and presents its own karmic challenges.

Other Homes- It is important to take note of the homes around your home site. Are the yards taken care of? If pets are in sight, do they look cared for? Are neighbors walking the neighborhood with ease or hurried? Is there a park nearby and, if so, is it well taken care of and used appropriately? Whether you are renting or buying, these are all questions to consider before moving into a neighborhood.

Notice the number of *For Sale* signs and even research the amount of turnover on the street. Is there an inordinate amount of foreclosures on the street or in the immediate area? Have homes been on the market for a longer-than-average amount of time? While a neighborhood may look pretty, if there is a lot of turnover or difficulty in selling homes, then that is a possible sign of a deeper, energetic problem going on with the land.

For example, a few years ago I did a feng shui consultation for a family that started experiencing a series of negative events as soon as they moved into their home. They were so disenfranchised with their home and situation that they were ready to move. The only problem was that there were so many other homes on their street that were either for sale or had been foreclosed upon that the value of their home was reduced to the point they couldn't afford to get out. So they decided to try feng shui. During the consultation, I discovered the problems were a combination of a faulty floor plan and an energetic toxicity that ran through the neighborhood. These issues combined with the occupants' overall negativity further spawned more negativity.

When I tapped into the land, I intuitively picked up that the land had been the site of slavery, abuse, and perhaps even massacre. What looked like any other suburban subdivision in America was the site of a darker energy that was still affecting residents centuries later. I cleared the home and land on which the house sat and instructed the occupants with what they could do to continue healing the home and the land.

In those cases where we find ourselves in a home containing a darker energy, it is our obligation to transmute the energy to a higher vibration. Even if you are without the knowledge or don't feel equipped to do it yourself, consider hiring a feng shui consultant or energy clearer. In doing so, you will help heal the home, the land, the planet, and yourself.

History of the Neighborhood- Just as it is important to learn as much about the history of your home before purchasing, so is the case with the neighborhood. In the example above, you can see how history continues to impact the neighborhood for decades, if not centuries, later. Patterns become set into the land and have a tendency to repeat themselves. Find out as much as you can about the area in which you live or desire to live.

Does the area have an affluent history? Was it the site of a Civil War battle? Is there a history of flooding, tornadoes, or other natural disasters? Have there been any incidents of toxic spills or higher rates of cancer? Was it the former site of a dump? I know that sounds extreme, but it happens. There is a large office park in Nashville built on top of a former landfill. According to rumors, discarded appliances will rear their heads on occasion.

Neighbors- Neighbors are a great indication of a neighborhood. Do neighbors seem happy? Is there an aliveness about the street or neighborhood? Are there positive indications, such as people strolling with babies, walking dogs, or riding bikes? Or do you hear loud music, cars, or, god forbid, yelling? Regardless of your neighborhood, you will most likely find yourself with less than perfect neighbors at some point. Like annoying coworkers, we are forced to mend fences and find a peaceful resolution. This is encouraged before resorting to moving. Otherwise, a similar situation will simply follow you to your next home.

Selecting a Home Site

Once you've found a general area or neighborhood that resonates with you, the next step is to find a house, lot, or unit that speaks to you. How the wind and water has shaped the land, the quality of soil, and movement or proximity of water was the original focus of feng shui in selecting sites for farming, abodes, rituals, burials, and even war thousands of years ago. Although conquering and settling new lands and territories isn't part of our modern-day life, selecting a location that fits our desired lifestyle is important.

Being conscious of our lot or home site often translates into dollar signs. While people may not think of it in terms of feng shui, there is a monetary price on lots depending on the feng shui of the land. Generally, homes in flood-prone areas are priced less than average. Homes sitting among rolling hills are generally considered favorable and come with a higher price tag. In most cities, it is the more affluent neighborhoods that are located in areas with the best feng shui. Even within a high-rise condo, the prices escalate the higher the floor a condo is located.

T-Intersections, Dead Ends, and Cul-de-Sacs

There are certain road configurations within subdivisions and neighborhoods that are not ideal due to the lack of flow created. For example, T-intersections create a line of energy, called a *poison arrow* in feng shui, that points sharply towards the house where the two streets meet. The same is true for dead-end streets. The best way to know whether this applies to you is if car headlights beam into your home at night. This rushing chi can lead to health issues, depletion of resources, and lethargy.

A tree or landscaping that blocks the point where the direct line of energy comes into the home is the best solution. While trees are generally not advised blocking the front door, this situation would be an exception. Hanging a wind chime over or around the front door is also recommended as it helps disperse the chi. Another remedy is to place a feng shui mirror over the front door or outside the home where the rushing chi reaches the home. This deflects the energy away from the home protecting it from the harmful energies, but should be used as a last resort.

Homes located at the end of a cul-de-sac or dead-end can experience similar issues and should be remedied accordingly as well. Homes at the end of a cul-de-sacs or dead-end should be avoided as they tend to collect stagnant chi. There is no flowing chi. Instead the energy stops coming to a "dead" end. If you live in a cul-de-sac or on a dead-end street, it is important to generate a flow of energy into your home. Using fountains, wind chimes, or birdbaths can stimulate the energy and help invite it into your home. Be sure to trim overgrown shrubs and avoid any yard clutter whatsoever. Ample outdoor lighting, colorful flowers, and a welcoming front door are also recommended.

The energy around your home cannot be underestimated in just how dramatically it can affect your destiny while living in your home. I have had many clients (including myself) that absolutely loved their home, but couldn't stay there due to issues surrounding their home. Usually, the issues will be compounded. For example, an underground disturbance on the land will set in motion certain patterns within the neighborhood, which then affects the types of neighbors and activities that occur.

In the case of one client, electromagnetic energy registered extremely high in a certain area of her bedroom when tested with a Trifield meter. There were no apparent electronics, wiring, or lines in or around the area and I never got to the source of the high level. Nevertheless, it is no coincidence that on that same side of the house attracted rude neighbors and car accidents.

In another case, a client purchased a foreclosed home in a desired subdivision. Immediately upon moving in, there were problems with the house. It got so bad that she and her husband referred to the home as "cursed." When I came to their home for a consultation, I noticed many feng shui problems all of which were remediable. However, when I looked behind the house, I instantly knew the source of the problem. The drainage system for the entire neighborhood ended in their backyard. The source of the problem was the land or lot itself. From the land, the problems trickled up into the home manifesting into feng shui issues and eventually wreaking havoc on its occupants.

Using Intuition

One of the best determinants of knowing whether a site or location will work for you is intuition. Intuition most often comes in the form of a sign, a feeling, or a visceral knowing. My client, Susan, walked up to look at a house and immediately noticed a dead black bird in the yard. She noted it to her husband as a bad sign about the house, but he discarded it as nothing. They signed a rental agreement on the home, but never finished out their lease. They were forced to leave the space early because it was completely contaminated and uninhabitable due to black mold underneath the house.

In another client situation, my client and I were viewing a Santa Monica condo. The property manager had cleared the time with the owner and knocked several times before entering. As we stepped into the living room, a woman came from nowhere and irately yelled, "YOU DO NOT BELONG HERE." My client and I looked at each other with a slight grin at how obvious the Universe had made it known that *he didn't belong here*. This condo was clearly not home.

These situations are great examples of watching for signs and trusting them. Omens or warnings could include dead birds or any type of dead animal around the premise, an unpleasant smell, a sudden headache or upset stomach, a rude neighbor appearing, or simply an odd or negative incident with someone walking by the house.

Positive signs might include finding a feather in the yard, feeling goose bumps as you enter the home, or simply a knowing that you are home. Just like meeting someone for the first time, your immediate first impression of a home is the most important. Often just driving up to a house or setting foot inside, you know you are home and want to stay or you know you want to leave. Trust your first impression. We often end up discounting our intuition because the home seems like a good deal or makes sense on paper.

Choosing a location will be the first and most important consideration you make in selecting a home. Do not underestimate the energetic implications of the land. By blending the tips from this section with your intuition, you will find the perfect spot on planet earth to support you and your family. If you're already settled in your home and it's not the ideal location, hopefully this chapter provided you with insights on optimizing your current property and locating your next home.

CHAPTER 2

YOUR HOME'S PERSONALITY - NUMEROLOGY

Geometry existed before the creation.

—**Plato**

Another consideration in choosing a home is its numerology. Beyond the blue shutters or soaring ceilings, each house has its own personality as unique as its occupants. The numerology of a space identifies its personality and how it will affect its occupants. Just like a relationship, a home will support you or, at times, challenge you.

Numbers are one of the oldest archetypal symbols and therefore carry a powerful energy. Interpretation of numbers is said to have preceded astrology and was used by the Ancient Mayans, the Mesopotamians, and Cabbalists, with Pythagoras being the first official numerologist. The Roman architect, Vitruvius, who is the subject of Leonardo Da Vinci's Vitruvian Man, was a proponent of the Sacred Geometry of Pythagoras and actually designed temples based on the proportions of the human body.

Numbers as Archetypes

Whole numbers are archetypes and the basis of a field known as numerology. I have always had a personal affinity and understanding of numbers from a young age. I can recall around age three when I was being taught numbers in pre-school. To help me remember them, I assigned a personality to each one of them as if numbers 1-9 were a large, extended family. It was only a few years ago as I was learning numerology when I realized my assigned characteristic of each number was in fact exactly consistent with its archetypal meaning. These archetypes or energies are part of our collective consciousness and part of the power that lies within numbers.

In numerology, all numbers are added up until you reach a single, whole number. It is the whole numbers 1-9 wherein you find the meaning. For example, the number *27* would hold the energy of a *9* (2+7). The number *123* would hold the energy of *6* (1+2+3). Each whole number has its own characteristic or meaning. Numerology is most commonly used on birthdates to determine personality characteristics and even life path divination. By assigning letters with a numerical value, numerology can also be done on names to determine certain personality traits.

Numerology for Homes

Numerology is also used for homes based on its street address. When a house is built, the lot is assigned a street number. This is usually considered its mailing address. The house immediately takes on the energy of that number. I often find that even the architecture of the house takes on the energy of the home's numerology. For example, a 3-House will often have a strong triangular shape, while a 4-House will have a solid square shape. Regardless however, the numerology will affect the overall energy of the home and directly affect its occupants.

Once you become familiar with the numerical energies, you can walk around your neighborhood and make a good guess as to the number represented before ever looking at the address by observing the architecture and exterior adornments made by the occupants. It's not necessary that the street number be posted on the house or mailbox for the house to take on the numerical energy. However, doing so can increase the power of that number even more so, especially if done with such an intention.

To determine the numerology for your home, simply add all of the digits of your street address together until you come up with a single digit. If you are familiar with numerology, it's the same formula, so to speak, to determine any numerical vibration. For example, if the address is 1539 Holly Street, then you would add the following:

$$1+5+3+9 = 18; \text{ then } 1+8 = 9$$

The house would therefore have the vibration of a *9*. If there is a number in the street name, you would not include it. For example, 123 2nd Street would still be a 6-House (1+2+3).

If an address includes a letter, for example, 4B, you would simply use the corresponding number to that letter, i.e. a = 1, b=2, c=3, etc., and add it just like a number (4+2 = 6).

A	B	C	D	E	F	G	H	I	J	K	L	M	N	O	P	Q	R	S	T	U	V	W	X	Y	Z
1	2	3	4	5	6	7	8	9	1	2	3	4	5	6	7	8	9	1	2	3	4	5	6	7	8

Like the numerology of your birthdate or name, so is the case with the numerology of your home. It will give you insight to the overall personality of your home. In my experience, the numerology of space is an accurate indicator of the energy of the home. The same is true with businesses. In fact, I find numerology of businesses to be an extremely important factor in the overall success and/or feel or branding of a business. By understanding the numerology of spaces, you can use it to make conscious decisions with regard to selecting a future home or business space.

For apartments or loft units within a building, you will have a number corresponding to the address of the building and one for your individual space. For example, if the address is: 923 Holly St. #402. The building would have the vibration of a "5" and the individual unit would have a "6" vibration. Both of these are information as to the energy of the space on a macro and micro level.

Below are the positive aspects and challenging aspects for each number to help you optimize your home's personality to support you as much as possible.

Number 1- The number *1* or a 1-House carries the frequency of unity, oneness, and new beginnings. A 1-House is perfect for a newly married couple. In fact, it holds a great energy to start anything new, such as s business, relationship, or self-improvement. It is a great house to express one's individuality and leadership skills in the world.

Of course, too much of anything is never good. Those living in a 1-House should be careful about not being too stubborn, domineering, or selfish. It's a great house to take care of *number 1*, metaphorically yourself, but be careful not to do so in excess. Other characteristics of a 1-House include being creative, original, and inventive.

With regard to businesses, it is a great space to bring people together in unity. It would be a great vibration for an office or home office for a creative entrepreneur coming up with new ideas and inventions. That being said, unless working in a group setting, feelings of isolation could set in.

Number 2- While a 1-House is great for individuation, a 2-House has a dualistic nature and is perfect for partnerships. The energy of harmony and a yin-yang balance is the predominant energy of the number 2. Whether it is business partners, lovers, or roommates, the 2-House inhabitants will be more agreeable and understanding, while also learning from each other.

The primary challenge with a 2-House is the tendency to become too sensitive to the other partner to the point where they end up not speaking their mind or sharing their opinion. Overall, however, the home will have a peaceful and harmonic balance. For a single person living in a 2-house, the home will naturally attract a partner for the occupant or provide the necessary growth to do so. It can also have the effect of longing for a partner. In business, it's a great office space or storefront for a business owned by business partners.

Number 3- The number "3" is known for its fun, extroverted energy, which also strikes a balance with its more spiritual properties. The number 3 is often depicted as a triangle, the trinity, or a pyramid, which is an energetic, fire-like quality lending itself to be very energetic. While the number 2 finds harmony and balance in twos, the number 3 finds balance in threes, similar to that of a tripod.

In metaphysical terms, it is associated with the triangular balance of mind body and spirit. A 3-House is often recognizable from the outside by having strong triangular rooflines. Three represents expression, expansion, passion, enthusiasm, extroverted, sexual energy, fun, and optimism. A 3-House is a great house for socializing and entertaining. It will have a positive energy and allow its occupants plenty of self-expression, literally in the home and also in the world. This is a great house for someone who wants to become more social, meet interesting people, and be visible.

The challenge in a 3-House is that it can be so much fun that not much work gets done. Spending too much money could also become an issue. It would be a challenging home to work from for introverted work, such as a writer or bookkeeper. However, it would be a great space for a party planner or events coordinator. I have also come across yoga studios in a 3-space. It is complimentary with the trinity balance of mind, body, spirit, but more conducive with the fiery nature of hot yoga rather than relaxing yoga or meditation.

Number 4- If feeling too scattered from living in a 3-House, then moving to a 4-House may be just what the doctor ordered. The number 4 has the energy of being stable, reliable, sturdy, grounded, organized, and productive. A 4-House will often be shaped like a sturdy box, similar to a four-square house. It is a great home or office space to start a new business or relationship. It provides a solid foundation on which to build.

A 4-House will also have the energy of Mother Earth and be very grounding for its occupants. It's a great space for someone who tends to be ungrounded, flighty, or has a hard time working on the physical plane. It can help with manifesting ideas into reality. The biggest challenge with a 4-House is that it can be all work and no play. It's important for the occupants to be conscious to build in playtime and avoid overworking themselves.

You can see how numbers 3 and 4 are virtually opposites of one another. This shows up throughout numerology. Numbers one and two are mirrors for one another as are three and four, five and six, seven and eight, and the number 9 being the grandmaster number. Each is the yin or yang for the other.

Number 5- A 5-House will embody the energy of activity, change, travel, adventure, and energy. It is a yang number that will always involve lots of movement and activity. In fact, the number 5 is the most energetic of all numbers and is most akin to the energy of change. When I see the numbers 555 together, for example, on a digital clock, I know that change is coming into my life and/or globally on the planet.

Both of the houses I grew up in were 5-Houses (113 and 131). It's not surprising, since my mother, who selected the homes, had lots of energy. Growing up, there was constant activity and lots of travel. This is the tell-tale sign of a 5-space. It can be like Grand Central Station with people coming and going. The number 5 also holds the energy of knowledge, communication, and writing, particularly regarding travel, other cultures, or new and interesting ideas.

The high energy of a 5-space can be challenging to feel settled and relaxed. It can create the tendency to move through life too quickly and be challenging to enjoy the present moment in a 5-house. A 5-space can be very good for a storefront as it will attract lots of foot traffic and stay busy.

Number 6- The number six holds the vibration of love, service, compassion, creativity, and artistry. A 6-House is truly a home with heart. This energy will be apparent in everything its inhabitants do from the arts to social responsibility. A 6-home is often recognizable by its exterior with an inviting front porch, a birdhouse in the tree for the animals, and perhaps some creative art in the front yard. It will often be the most artistic and cozy house on the block.

A 6-House is a great home in which to raise a family as you will often see a 6-House filled with children. On the social scene, while wild raucous parties take place in the 3-House, the 6-House will host the intimate dinner party with friends while sharing stories of traveling to orphanages in Africa. Artfully prepared food and wine from a visited winery will accompany the meal.

Inhabitants of a 6-House love their home so much that their biggest challenge is to not become reclusive. Another challenge is that the home can be so heart-oriented that it can be a challenging home for material success. It would not be complimentary to someone whose objective is to make lots of money. However, it would be perfect for someone who wants to be more in touch with their heart and passions in life, which of course can lead to much success. It is a great home in which to have a service-based business, particularly one that is heart-based. With regard to a business, it is best for office space with healing-based practitioners, such as psychotherapists, chiropractors, or other healers.

Number 7- The number 7 is the most spiritual of all numbers. It appears in the Bible and in many religions and cultures and therefore carries the energy of spirituality, mysticism, philosophy, introspection, and solitude. A 7-House is likened to an ashram, temple, or sanctuary. It feels very calm, peaceful, relaxing, quiet, zen, and, in some cases, slightly cave-like. It holds the energy of deep, spiritual transformation.

About 85% of the time I come across a 7-House it's inhabited by a single woman undergoing a transformative time of life. Because of its mysticism and inward energy, the 7-House is also very conducive to honing one's intuitive or psychic abilities. It holds a yin energy and can lend itself to a more inward lifestyle with few social connections with the exception of a few, deep friendships. It is a great space for someone focused on their spiritual growth.

The challenge is getting out of the house and feeling a part of the world. Because it is so spiritual based, it can be challenging to operate in the physical confines of the 3D physical world. It is advisable for those living in a 7-House to make a conscious effort to get out of the house and connect with others. It would not be the best house for an introvert who would benefit from a social life.

A 7-House can sometimes be challenging for a couple. Because the home is so transformative, a couple will either grow together, thereby bringing them closer, or grow apart. Of course, the positive side of that is that it will fast track a relationship in the direction it needs to go. For a family or household living in a 7-House, religion or spirituality will play an important role in the home. With regard to businesses, I rarely come across a business located in a 7-space. I would have some concern for a storefront business that is in a 7-space, but it would be ideal for a church or a meditative space.

Number 8- If you are looking for material success or wealth, the 8-House is for you. While the 7-House rules the spiritual plane, the 8-House rules the physical plane. The 8-House can bring abundance in every area, whether in the form of love or money. Eight holds the vibration of success, power, infinity, fortune, and fame. Even the 8-House itself can bring wealth in the real estate market. Also don't be surprised to receive public recognition, or even fame when living in an 8-House. Of course, all of this does not come without hard work, which the 8-House also supports by way of its vibration of power and leadership.

In Chinese metaphysics, the number 8 is the most auspicious. In China, it is common for homes with the numerology of 8 sell for considerably more money for this very reason. The number eight by virtue of its shape of the infinity symbol is a special number. The challenge with the 8-House is to not become so caught up in the material world to where one would lose focus on matters of the heart.

Number 9- The number 9 holds the energy for completion. And, with any ending, there is also a new beginning. Nine holds the vibration of generosity, giving, loving, wisdom, compassion, and representative of light workers. The 9-House is a great house for someone who is wrapping up a major phase of his or her life. I often see clients in a 9-House move away to another city or some other transitory time of life.

The 9-House is supportive for ending a phase of life, allowing for a complete release in order to start anew, or finally closing a business deal. In the case of one client, she rented a 9-House following the break-up with her fiancé. In releasing this relationship, she also cleaned up her finances and cleaned out tons of old storage items. She was then able to move on, in fact to a 6-House, where she had a thriving healing practice giving to others her love and compassion. The 9-House will help wrap up those loose ends of completion.

The 9-House is also associated with humanitarianism and service. The primary challenge of a 9-House is to not let others take advantage of your generosity. It is also important to take care of yourself while saving the world. A 9-space would be ideal for a shelter, a nonprofit, or other humanitarian-based business, especially if related to healing the past.

Number 11 and 22- I once had a client who was having serious marital issues. She and her husband had been separated for over a year with both still living in the same house. She said that they both loved the house so much that it was the main reason that they had not permanently separated and divorced. When I asked what her address is, it was no surprise that they were living in an 11-house. Homes with the energy of "11" are extremely powerful, intuitive, and almost magical. In fact, I rarely, if ever, visit an 11-home where the owners don't absolutely love their home. This is an example of the power of numbers.

While you would continue adding the numbers until you come up with a single digit, the numbers 11 and 22 are considered master numbers. As I mentioned, the number 11 is a special number that makes for a special home. An 11-House will have very little turnover in the real estate market. It will not only have the energy of a 2-House, but also that of an 11-House.

The number "11" is considered to be a master number with a special energy. As I mentioned earlier, an 11-House holds an almost magical energy. You can usually spot an 11-House walking down the street. It will sit naturally on its lot and have an irresistible charm. The number 11 holds the energy of intuition, psychic abilities, and perhaps creates a portal for angelic presence. The number 22, while also being a 4, holds the energy of mastery.

You might be wondering if the numerology of your home is the best fit for you. Maybe you live in a 5-House and can never sit still. Or perhaps you are in a 7-House and are having difficulty meeting new people. Generally speaking, the home we are attracted to has an energetic resonance with us. This resonance may be out of habit or it could be a subconscious knowing of what is best for our soul's evolution. For example, the very first home I purchased out of law school was a 5-House which was the same energy I had grown up with. While that didn't really fit my energy or what I really needed in hindsight, the energy was an energetic resonance with the pattern I had grown up with. Having awareness of what space best supports us instead of falling into default patterns is an example of living more consciously.

You can now consciously take into account the numerology when selecting spaces for future homes and businesses. For example, after living in an 8-House for several years, I needed to reconnect to my heart and passion in life. I knew a 6-House would be a perfect fit. Shortly thereafter, I noticed a house I had always loved was on the market. It just so happened to be a 6-House. I immediately called my realtor. When I got her email that said, "the house has been on the market for 66 days.

I will meet you there at 3:30," I smiled and thanked the Universe for its confirmation.

If you find yourself in a house with numerology that is not serving you positively, then there are ways to counteract this. Some feng shui consultants recommend adding a letter or number to energetically alter the home's numerology. In my opinion, this is like asking someone to wear a mask covering up who they truly are. Instead, I would advise making conscious efforts to shift one's own energy within the house.

For example, if you live in a 5-House and want more peace and relaxation, then carve out a meditation space in the house. Or if you live in a 4-House, then consciously host more dinner parties. If you live in a 3-House and find that you are spending too much money, then devise a budget and work on sticking to it. Sometimes having the opposing energy will bring in more awareness to transforming the challenge into a positive.

CHAPTER 3

YOUR HOME'S BODY - THE SHAPE OF THE HOUSE AND HOW IT SHAPES YOU

Life begins well, it begins enclosed, protected, all warm in the bosom of the house.

—Gaston Bachelard, *The Poetics of Space*

Not only does a home's numerology affect its personality and therefore its occupants, but so does the shape of the house. The shape of a house has been likened to the shape of the human face for centuries. The windows are the eyes; the front door is the mouth; and the roof being the head. Beyond the typical structure of a house, there are as many shapes of houses as there are body types. The shape of a house will greatly affect the energy of the house and have an impact upon its occupants. While a square or rectangle house is the most common and auspicious shape in feng shui, you have to look deeper. For example, a wide rectangular ranch house has a very different energy than a long rectangular shotgun house.

Do you live in a single-story ranch, a multi-story home, or a 5th floor condominium? Or perhaps you are renting the basement space of a house or an attic? Not only does the shape of a house impact its occupants, so does the space in which you specifically inhabit. The overall floor structure or shape of a house and where you live within the space is directly connected with where your focus or growth will take place while living in that particular house.

For example, if your house is only one level, then your focus while living in that house will primarily take place in day-to-day life at your present level of consciousness. On the other hand, someone living in a house with a large, roomy attic may find themselves working through belief systems to expand their spirituality and higher state of consciousness. A house with a large basement for storage will lend itself to storing items and therefore emotions. Meanwhile, a home with no basement may force its owners to face the past and deal with old emotions that haven't been processed.

We are ultimately attracted to the house that is a vibrational match to us. The shape of the house is integral to this. It is not uncommon for a couple having their first child to move to a different shape of house entirely. As their lifestyle changes, so does the shape of their home. Not only does expansion in the size of the house mirror the size of the family, but the number of stories and where the bedrooms are located on those floors becomes paramount. Ranch-style homes emerged with overwhelmingly popularity during the 1950's baby boom. The one-level ranch puts the focus on the routine of everyday family living with all bedrooms on the same floor.

Consider the shape of the house you currently live in compared to your previous homes. Do you see a pattern? During one of my moves, I went from a cozy single-story home with a large basement to a tall, two-story home with only a crawl space. With two floors of tall ceilings, a roomy attic, and a high roofline, it not only felt physically expansive, but also proved to be spiritually expansive as well.

Take a moment to think about the levels of your home. Do you live in a single or multi-story home? What level do you spend most of your time on? How does it differ from your previous homes? You can usually start to see a correlation between the houses you have lived in and your life situation at that time.

For example, living in a single-story house may have allowed you to focus on the present, perhaps while in college or raising a family. Did you experience a spiritual awakening in the multi-story home with a roomy attic? Or did it reveal old patterns that needed clearing that were no longer serving you? Often, after living in a two-story home people want to move to a one-level home for practical reasons. And for others who have been living in a one-level home, the expansion of multi-stories is freeing. Like relationships, we often seek the opposite traits from what we previously experienced.

Childhood Home

As we burst out of the womb and into this big world, our home becomes our first line of defense, second only to our crib. Our home is our safe place. For this reason, we often unconsciously replicate our childhood home years later as we become adults. We are naturally attracted to a similar shape of house and in some cases even a similar floor plan as the home we grew up in. Because it was our safe place as a child, we find the energy of a similar home familiar, comfortable, and safe. We go back to that which is familiar, especially when/if the time comes to have children of our own. A couple may disagree in their search for a house as each one is unknowingly attempting to replicate their own childhood experience.

Even if you lived in many different homes growing up, there is most likely one home in particular that you consider your "childhood home." Think back to the floor plan of that home. Do you see similarities in your childhood home and homes you've lived in since?

Too Little, Too Big, or Just Right?

Our energy field shrinks or expands in accordance with its surroundings. When you walk into a building, your subconscious mind begins roaming around and exploring every nuance of the space. If you feel safe, your energy field expands into the space a little more as you get comfortable. In our home, our energy field continues to expand into the entire space as we settle in.

Think of a plant growing in a glass box. It will continue to grow until it rubs up against the walls. If the box is too small, it might even start to bend in order to keep growing. Place a plant in a tall, skinny box and it will grow tall and skinny. If a plant were in a long, wide box, then it would grow out wide. The same is true for our energy in our home. It will take the shape of the box - our home. This is also the reason that spaces built with sacred geometry feel good to be in. Our energy field, which is also based upon sacred geometry, fills the space. It is like beautiful music rather than a missed chord.

Have you ever felt at some point in your life that you have outgrown a space, maybe to the point of even feeling claustrophobic? Your energy field is literally rubbing up against the walls and craving expansion. In big cities, such as New York City where spaces are tiny, most city dwellers will tell you that they spend very little time at home. Because the city itself is so expansive, they are able to expand their energy beyond a 400-square foot apartment. When they come home to sleep, the space feels more like a protective nest. Nevertheless, when space is a premium it is important to be discriminating about every piece of furniture and item you have in the space. Clutter only takes up more space and causes the walls to feel more closed in.

When I conducted workshops in New York City, not having enough space was a prevalent theme. Interestingly however, the week before my trip to New York, all of the clients I was seeing in Nashville were struggling with the opposite problem - too much space. Yes, it is possible to have too much space. A space that is too big stretches your energy field too much and too thin and perhaps your wallet too. You will feel scattered, unsettled, and often unsafe. I had one client in this predicament. As she was furnishing the unused rooms, she realized she was just "staging" her own home. It was not her energy in those rooms. By moving to a smaller space, she was able to gather

her energy back and use it in a more focused way rather than feeling scattered.

A similar problem happens sometimes with couples moving from a small, cozy space into a large, expansive home. As soon as they move into the larger space, they start having marital problems. The expansion of their energy in the new home takes them in different directions. You can also see this with businesses sometimes that move into a larger space in order to accommodate more business just to have their business drop off as soon as they do. The expansion of energy is too much too soon and they lose themselves and their identity.

All rooms should have an identity and purpose. Otherwise, you are underutilizing aspects of yourself. If you completely run out of ideas for a room, then it is possible that your home is too large for you. Avoid using unused spaces to store clutter. Storage is different than clutter. Storage is storing items that still serve a defined purpose and function for you. Clutter is stuff that you no longer love or use that drains your energy or keeps you stuck in the past. On the other hand, if you feel your space is so small that it is inhibiting you from exploring new aspects of yourself, such as art, music, sewing, or starting a family, then you may have outgrown your current space and it may be time to upgrade to a larger space.

Windows and natural light can alter the energy in a space and allow for more expansion. For my 9th-grade science project, I planted three plants -- one upright, one sideways, and one upside down. All three grew up toward the light defying gravity. This is similar to how our energy responds to natural light. Having windows and natural light in our space is crucial to our energy field. Areas of the home with the most natural light are usually the most used rooms and where our energy is most present in the home. Windows allow our energy to expand beyond the walls. Simply by looking out a window, we expand. Where intention goes, energy flows. However, windows can be an energy drain at night and should be covered, especially in rooms and bedrooms being used.

Grounding In

In order to spread our wings and expand in all areas of your life, it is essential that we ground into the earth. In continuing with the analogy of a tree, the deeper a tree's roots, the higher it can grow. This is the case with our personal energy as well. In order to grow and expand in life, we have to be grounded and rooted in our energy. Otherwise, success can turn into disaster. You can see this with child stars and other celebrities who suddenly become famous. If energy isn't grounded, it will fly away. We all know someone who seems flighty, spacey, or in the clouds. They may access profound ideas and information, but they are not grounded enough to actually manifest anything in physical form. On the flip side, there are those who are too grounded and get stuck and stagnant in their life.

Spaces also embody these energy patterns based on their shape. For example, a home with a deep basement dug out of the ground will be more grounding than a home on the edge of a cliff built on stilts. The closer you are physically to the Earth, the more grounded you will feel. The deeper a foundation is dug out for a home, the closer and more in tune with the Earth its occupants will be. It will be a supportive space, particularly to people who need more grounding energy.

It would not surprise me if less turnover occurs in homes with basements as opposed to those built on slabs or even crawl spaces. This can vary regionally as well depending on the topography the area. Occupants are more likely to settle and ground into the home itself. They will feel an innate connection with the Earth, even if not consciously aware of why. Think back on your homes and whether they had basements, or not. Was there a correlation with your connection to that home? Did you happen to live there for a longer period of time?

Even within a home, the energy can change depending on what floor you primarily live or work, i.e. basement, main level, or attic space. Living in a basement is ill-advised, at least not for very long. Humans are not meant to live below ground. When you hear of horrific things happening in a home, it's not coincidental that it's often in the basement. As discussed in greater detail in Chapter 9, the basement represents the subconscious mind and can become a storehouse of emotions from the past.

Compare homes with a basement to the complete opposite - a high-rise condo. Condos are not very grounding and usually attract people who travel a lot, in transition, or those with an active social life. It also attracts people who don't want to maintain a yard, thereby making the space even less grounding. In the architecture classic, *A Pattern Language*, it is recommended that no building be built over four stories. Clearly, builders have overlooked this suggestion as living spaces continue to be built higher and higher.

On the other hand, there can be a beneficial energy that can also come with an ungrounded space. The occupants do not feel "tied down." It allows a sense of freedom, exploration, change, inventiveness, creativity, and an overall active lifestyle. There may be a time in one's life when this is an attractive and serving energy. For example, some empty-nesters love urban, high-rise living after the responsibilities of raising a family in a single-family home for most of their lives.

On the flip side, couples who have enjoyed urban, condo living may end up moving to a home "to settle down" with a family. You can see the contrast in lifestyle and how spaces can support these differences. For those living in a high-rise condo and struggling with feeling ungrounded, it is advisable to find a unit with the numerology of the number 4. Although high in the sky, its numerology will help ground the space.

What Architectural Style is Best for You?

Because the shape of your house plays a role in shaping your life, you may be wondering what shape of house is best for you. Similar to fashion trends, we often want the next best thing with regard to interior finishes. Trends in architecture, however, are not as changeable. Instead, location will usually determine the architectural style we choose based on the type of neighborhood we are attracted to.

In urban neighborhoods, you will see a throwback to past eras in architectural styles with original Victorians, Craftsmen Bungalows, and Four Squares. These are often mixed with apartments and mixed-use condo spaces. These neighborhoods tend to attract a younger demographic wanting to enjoy the amenities of living close to work, restaurants, and retail.

In newer, suburban neighborhoods, more traditional styles, such as Colonial and Traditional two-story homes are prevalent. Similar to its architect styles, the lifestyle in these areas tends to be more traditional as well. In between these two worlds, you will find 1950 ranch-style homes, mid-century moderns, and newly-built modern homes. Let's take a look at each in more detail.

Victorians- Victorians in the United States were built in the late 1800s and early 1900s. There are various styles of Victorians, such as Italianate, Gothic, and Queen Anne. Each have their own distinct touches, but all Victorians are ornately built with lots of architectural detail. They were built to impress and known for their unique character and charm. And so will be true for those who live in a Victorian home.

Our home is always a reflection of ourselves, and their personality will almost always mirror its owners. Those who live in Victorian homes will be full of character and charm themselves, perhaps even bordering on eccentricity in some cases. The more detailed the architecture elements of the home, the more detail-oriented its occupants will be.

Victorians are known for their grand entrances and staircases, towers and turrets, high ceilings, and often a wide hallway. The sky is the limit for its occupants as well with being blessed with many opportunities. On the other hand, Victorians built with choppy rooms, dark and narrow hallways, and with lots of clutter can lead to a lack of energy or depression. Its occupants could also feel scattered in too many directions depending on how elaborate the home is. Becoming mired in details to the point of missing the big picture is another challenge of those living in a Victorian home.

Craftsman and American Bungalows- Starting in California and spreading east, Craftsman-style homes were the next trend after the Victorian movement in the early 1900s. As a stark contrast to the Victorian-style home, the Craftsman style was built upon the principles of using space efficiently, closer to Earth, and with practicality. And so is the case with those who choose to live in a Craftsman or Bungalow-style home.

The Craftsman house is known for its coziness, often built lower to the ground with deep eaves, with an emphasis on wood accents throughout. A large front porch makes the home welcoming and accessible to neighborhood living. It has a more open floor plan than a Victorian with lots of windows. It also borrows from the minimalism of Japanese zen style of architecture, leaving the space feeling much more clean-lined and clutter-free than the Victorian. This style is more about practicality and simplicity rather than the showiness of the Victorian era.

It's not surprising that there has been a re-emergence of this style over the past decade. Entire subdivisions are borrowing from the Craftsman and Bungalow style, recreating neighborhoods from the early 1900's. As trends have moved toward organic, earth materials, and minimalism, the Craftsman style goes hand-in-hand with that aesthetic. Craftsman and Bungalows are very grounding homes, and occupants often feel "at home" in that cozy environment.

Shotgun House- One of the most identifiable shapes, with its shape narrow width and deep length, is the Shotgun-style House or row house. The Shotgun House originated in the South, particularly in New Orleans and hot climates to facilitate a breeze throughout the house. Although originally a symbol of poverty, the Shotgun style is still used in new construction today due to its adaptable shape, particularly in urban areas where lots are narrow.

The Shotgun house is typically built with the front door lined up directly with the back door and open all the way through. This floor plan is disfavored in feng shui as the energy enters the home and escapes quickly out the backdoor. Ironically, the name shotgun is said to originate from a shotgun being able to shoot from the front door all the way out the back. This is a perfect analogy for how the energy enters and immediately escapes the home with this floor plan.

The shape of the shotgun house gives its occupants privacy from the outside world. It is an important factor if considering living in a shotgun-shaped home. I once lived in a house that was shaped similar to a shotgun house. I suppose we should have seen the writing on the wall when we actually found a shotgun in the yard the day we moved in. Because the neighborhood had safety issues, the shotgun shape felt protective from the street with the main living spaces being at the back of the home.

Ranch-Style- The ranch-style home originated in the United States in the 1920s and really boomed in post-war 1950s. This style is particularly known for its long, low-to-the-ground shape with few exterior or interior elements. Its style was born out of the merging of the mid-century modern homes and casual western ranch homes. It therefore has a relaxed, casual feel mixed with a sense of minimalism. Its occupants will embody these personality traits as well.

The popularity of ranch homes grew out of their ease and affordability. The style functioned to serve a wide variety of socio-economic levels. As a result, the ranch-style home can be found in lower economic areas, as well as more affluent neighborhoods. Similar to the reemergence of Craftsman-style homes, ranch homes have caught the attention of younger generations, particularly those generations that did not live in them the first go-around. Due to their minimalistic shell exterior and affordability, they are ripe for renovating, extending, and morphing into just about anything.

Due to their low-to-the-ground façade, ranch-style homes are grounding and allow the occupants to feel close to the outdoors and nature. Unless renovated, they are generally one-story and shaped like a long rectangle. This puts the focus on the trials and tribulations of everyday living for the occupants. Due to its practicality and functionality, it makes a great home for family living with everyone being on the same floor.

Mid-Century Modern- Mid-century modern is an entire movement that took root in architecture, graphics, and furniture design during the mid-twentieth century in California. It is a style that is still alive and well today. Mid-century moderns have similar elements as Craftsmans, such as clean lines and an emphasis on bringing earth elements in. However, mid-centuries bring a more modern aesthetic with influences from Scandinavian and German Bauhaus architects. On the interior an emphasis was placed on family life with the goal of modernizing the suburban family. Even today, you will see occupants in these homes as forward-thinking modernists interested in design, fashion, art, and green design.

Traditional- Traditional, also known as American, is the most common style of home found throughout the United States and Canada. It is a sort of hodge-podge of styles with an emphasis on fitting the functionality of today's families. Traditional homes can be found as one or two-story homes. Large, two-story versions of the Traditional-style, often referred to as McMansions, have come to epitomize standardized living in the United States. A front porch is usually built to be a transitional space into the home rather than for sitting and connecting with neighbors. Exterior elements borrow from other styles of homes and are usually consistent within a defined subdivision.

The interior is built around the kitchen and living room as the center of the home with bedrooms either on the periphery or upstairs. Home offices, bonus rooms, family rooms, TV rooms, and game rooms are popular features to fit a modern-day family lifestyle. Being the most popular style, occupants are typically in the prime of their lives with a busy family life. With the emphasis on the practical, the home serves as a tool to make life easier, quicker, comfortable, and accommodating to kids and families.

Duplex- Duplex homes originated during the Great Depression and World War II era as the federal government were stimulating the housing industry with tax deductions for mortgage interest. Duplexes were attractive because they made housing even more affordable than renting. Unfortunately, however, not only do homeowners only own half of the house, but only embody half of the energy as well.

Occupants of duplex homes will be challenged with balance and embodying their full energy. They may feel like they are missing some aspect of their life and not completely 'whole' in some way. That being said, it could strengthen certain aspects - perhaps the right-brain, creative side or the left-brain, analytical side - by putting a focus on that one area. For this reason, duplexes are best utilized as temporary spaces to allow its occupants to focus on certain areas of their lives for a short amount of time.

Old Home or New Home

Old homes and new homes alike come in all different styles. But beyond the style of home, whether you live in an older home or new home takes on a different energy. Some people are attracted to turn-of-the-century homes for the character or craftsman quality. Others may feel more comfortable in a 1950's era ranch with its cozy, down-home feel. Many people prefer a brand new home to start fresh with everything working properly and no predecessor energy to worry about. And still others may prefer a newer home without having to add the sweat equity touches of window treatments and landscaping. Regardless of your preference, the age of the house you choose is not coincidental. It is indicative of a bigger picture.

Similar to starting a "new" year, a newly constructed house can be the beginning of a new phase in one's life. It may mark the beginning of a new marriage, a new baby, or perhaps moving to a smaller, new house once the kids are out of the house. Whatever the life circumstance is, it will mark a significant new beginning. If you have ever moved into a newly constructed home, think back to what phase of life was transpiring.

In contrast, have you ever bought an older home in need of a renovation? It was probably at a time in which you were going through a renovation, or rebuilding, of yourself. Living in a home being renovated will most likely occur at a time of transition. From age four through twenty-nine, with a few exceptions in my college years, I had always lived in a new home. After I went through a divorce, I moved into an old home for the first time. An old house represents your old beliefs, attitudes and how you used to think or feel. I needed to update my mode of thinking. My old belief systems no longer worked for me. This house gave me the opportunity to completely transform my life.

Older homes can provide the best backdrop for your own personal renovation, or transformation. As changes or renovations are made to the house, the correlating transformation will be reflected in the homeowner. Consider a time in which you have renovated, remodeled, or simply redecorated a room. And then consider what you were experiencing in your life at that time. Was it a job or even career change, personal relationship issue, a change in belief system, or any number of things? This is another example of your home being a mirror of your life.

CHAPTER 4

YOUR HOME'S PATH - FLOOR PLAN OF THE HOUSE

Architecture is basically a container of something. I hope they will enjoy not so much the teacup, but the tea.

—Yoshio Taniguchi

Thus far we have seen how the exterior of the house affects the energy of a space. Now we will shift to the interior of the home, starting with the floor plan. While the shape of the house provides a big picture of the energy of the home, the floor plan fills in the canvas and paints a more detailed picture. Similar to one's astrology chart or the palm of the hand, your home's floor plan will determine to some degree your path while living there. It will reveal what areas of your life will be under a spotlight while living there. The floor plan of a house will support you in some areas and potentially challenge you in others.

When I visit someone's home for a feng shui consultation, I can tell a lot about the lives of the occupants simply by looking at their floor plan. I notice if and where there is a missing corner or an extension; the overall flow of energy throughout the home; where the energy feels cut off; and where the bathrooms are located. I notice where the staircases are located. I notice how the energy comes in through the front door and where it flows from there. I notice which rooms are clearly the homeowners' favorite versus least favorite. All of these factors tell a story of what is going on in their life.

Usually there is an imbalance of energy throughout a home consistent with the floor plan that mirrors the imbalance of the homeowners. By shifting the energy with feng shui adjustments, space clearing, and/or intention, areas of the home that were stagnant or cut off from the flow suddenly have new, fresh energy. As a result, the home is brought into balance and corresponding changes will start to take place in their life. Let's take a closer look.

Flow of Energy

Like streams and rivers, the energy should meander throughout your home. Spaces will feel best when the energy is in harmony or most similar to the natural flow of the Earth's energy, which is consistent with sacred geometry. The word *meander* is a term that is commonly used in feng shui and best describes how energy should ideally flow. Energy should not stagnate, nor should it be rushing. It should meander. As it does, it collects the beneficial chi and keeps it gently moving throughout the space. This is a balanced energy and will help the occupants feel relaxed, yet energetic, at the same time. At the same time, the entire space will receive a balanced energy throughout.

The overall flow of your home will largely depend upon your floor plan. As the builders start putting up walls into a space, the energy starts shifting. Walls direct energy where to go and where not to go. Clearly, without them, there would just be a big empty box with four exterior walls and a roof. It is the walls that move, shift, direct, and collect energy. Doors and windows are built into walls and further direct the energy in spaces.

Doorways connect rooms and help energy flow from room to room. They should therefore be strategically placed throughout the space to allow for a meandering, smooth flow of energy. Interior doors provide an integral function in a home to connect spaces and create boundaries when needed. Windows connect the space to the rest of the world. Windows are the eyes of the home and allow the occupants to feel a connection to nature, other people, the city, or whatever environment the space is located.

Do's and Don'ts for Interior Door Placement

- Avoid placing doors that bang against one another when they open as this can lead to conflict among the occupants.
- Avoid doors opening into a wall as opposed to into the room.
- Avoid placing doors where they cannot fully open. Also do not store items behind doors.
- Avoid too many doors lined up in a row, i.e. three or more doors lined down a hallway.
- Fix or remove broken doors as this can hinder opportunities and lead to health issues.
- If two doors are across from each other, have them aligned directly across from one another as opposed to overlapping one another.

The Bagua Map

Another way to determine how your life will be affected by your home's floor plan is with the Bagua Map. The Bagua Map is a tool used in feng shui used to determine where certain areas of your life fall within your home. The Bagua Map is a nine-sectioned square or rectangle, similar to a tic-tac-toe board and arranged with the architecture-intended front of the home. In some feng shui schools, the map is octagonal in shape and applied using compass directions.

Each square or section of the Bagua Map is called a *gua* and associated with a specific trigram from the *iChing*. The *iChing* translates to the *The Book of Changes* and is considered to be one of the oldest books. It originated in China and contains a set of oracular statements consisting of 64 sets of six lines, called hexagrams, commonly used as a divination tool. A solid line represents *yang* energy, while a broken line represents *yin* energy.

The specific arrangement of the guas holds a mystical quality that can be applied to virtually any space, including a floor plan, an individual room, a desk, a vision board, and even your car. This arrangement has also been indoctrinated into our collective consciousness, similar to dream symbols. Think of each one of these areas as energy portals underneath your home from which you can access energy or support. The goal is to unblock these energy centers, bring them into balance, and enhance if needed. The energy of each of these guas is present in your home and is yours to harness, balance, and utilize to your benefit, especially when combined with our personal intentions of these nine areas of your life.

ABUNDANCE & PROSPERITY	FAME & REPUTATION	LOVE & RELATIONSHIPS
FAMILY & COMMUNITY	MIND BODY & SPIRIT	CREATIVITY & CHILDREN
WISDOM & SELF-AWARENESS	CAREER & LIFE PURPOSE	HELPFUL PEOPLE & TRAVEL

⊢──────── front entrance ────────⊣

The instructions for applying the Bagua Map are in accordance with the more western versions of feng shui. As opposed to orienting the Bagua Map based upon compass directions, the alignment is based upon how the human energy is intended to come into the space, which is through the front door. Simply line the bottom edge of the Bagua Map with the front wall of your home. This is usually the same wall that your front door is on or the architecture-intended front of the home. If you are unclear as to where the front of your home is, it usually faces the street of your address. If your front door is centered on the front of your home, you will be walking into the *Career & Life Purpose* section. The area in the back-left corner of your home is your *Wealth & Prosperity* section, and so forth.

FAQs for Applying the Bagua Map

- **Do I include my garage?** Yes, include everything attached that is under roof, including garages.
- **What about porches, decks and patios?** If it is not under roof, then it is not included in the Bagua Map. Instead, those areas would be considered 'extensions' of the gua they are coming off of. For example, if you have a deck in the back middle of your home, it is an extension of your Fame & Reputation section. These architectural features can be helpful for filling in missing corners, as discussed below.
- **What if my front door is on the side of my house?** This is rare, but does happen occasionally, especially with condos and townhomes. You will align the Bagua Map with the front wall of the house. If you live in an apartment or condo unit, you will align it with the door coming into your space. If the front is still not obvious, then the side of the house that intuitively seems like the front of the house or intended by the architect. Often, it will face the street from which you enter.
- **What about other stories of my home?** For multi-story homes, the Bagua Map will be the same for each floor as if stacking the Bagua Map on top of the other.

- **What about walls?** Ignore walls when orienting the Bagua Map. For example, your kitchen may be in your Wealth Corner and Fame Corner. Or your Wealth Corner may contain only part of a room.
- **What if the functions of the room don't match up with the Bagua Map?** That's okay. Rarely will your bedroom be in your Love & Relationships Corner and your home office be in your Wealth Corner. Your Love Corner may be in your garage or bathroom. Either way, that is your Love Corner.
- **What if a section or part of a section is cut-out or missing on my floorplan?** This is referred to as a 'missing corner' in Feng Shui. Bad news is that that section of your home is missing. Good news is that there are remedies.

Bagua Map Analysis

For each section of the Bagua Map, consider the following questions:

- What room(s) are within this section?
- Go to this area of your home. Look around objectively as if it's someone else's home. What jumps out at you, positively or negatively?
- Does this area seem to flow or feel constricted? Does it feel like there are too many pieces of furniture or too little?
- What is your **FAVORITE** part about this area of your home?
- What is your **LEAST** favorite part about this area of your home? i.e. color, furniture, layout, clutter, pictures, function, etc.
- Are there any items that conjure up old memories? If so, are the memories happy, sad, bitter, sweet, guilty, regretful, resentment, or feel stagnant in any way?
- Are there cluttered zones within this area? i.e. drawers, closets, cabinets, pantry?

Missing Corners

Most homes are not a perfect square or rectangle and therefore have either a *missing corner* or *extension* in feng shui. A missing corner will look like a bite out of your floor plan that is less than fifty percent of the entire wall. Whereas an extension looks like an elongated area extending from the floor plan that is less than fifty percent of the length of the wall. For an L-shaped home, the wall is exactly fifty percent creating either a missing corner or an extension depending on your preference.

If you have an extension of one of the guas, then that area of your life will be highlighted while living there. For example, my client, Cindy, had a large extension of her Love & Relationships corner. During the entire six years she lived there, her love life was her primary focus and the area of significant personal growth. Unfortunately, however, it can lead to an imbalance on one's overall wellbeing. When a certain area of your life is highlighted, it can lead to deficiency in other areas. So once again, the ideal shape for optimum grounding and balancing is a square or rectangular-shaped house.

If you have a missing corner, then the energy associated with that section will be energetically missing from your home and therefore your life. This can lead to challenges or struggles in that area of your life. Most missing corners tend to show up on the back area of the house, particularly in the Love and Money corners. Not surprising that love and money tend to be the two areas we as a society struggle with the most. If it is your Wealth corner, then you may be financially challenged while living in that space. Even if money is flowing in, it could flow out even quicker or you could simply struggle with a lack mindset toward money.

The Bagua Map can be used as sparingly or extensively as you prefer. I have witnessed significant changes in my clients' lives in using the Bagua Map by placing their energy, focus, and intention in the desired areas in which they want to make changes. By clearing clutter and bringing in certain colors, elements, remedies, and intentions, transformation will happen.

The good news about feng shui is that there is a remedy for just about anything. And so is the case with missing corners. In fact, you could turn a negative into a positive. It's possible to put so much energy and attention into remedying a missing corner that that area of life can flourish as a result.

Here are some ways to remedy the missing area to create a square or rectangle floor plan:

> **Work From the Exterior-** Add landscaping or ornamental features in the missing corner, such as a patio, bushes, flowers, birdbath, and/or chimes. Fill the space in with lighting. With solar lighting so accessible, this can be an easy and inexpensive way to fill in a missing corner.
>
> **Work From the Interior-** If the exterior is not accessible, for example, in a condo, then you can fill in a missing corner from the inside of your space. Work with one of the two walls (or both) that create the missing corner. If one or both of the walls has a window, then the missing corner is already being remedied. The window helps to expand the energy out into the missing space.

If you do not have a window on one of the walls, the next best remedy is to place a mirror on one of the walls. In this case, the mirror will energetically extend the wall out similar to a window. Another option is to add a piece of artwork, preferably a landscape. Place or hang a crystal anywhere in that area to further balance the energy.

Front Door

The front door of the home is the primary vessel through which energy enters a space. In feng shui, the front door is referred to as the *primary mouth of chi*. For this reason, it is important that the front door be obvious and welcoming. Have you ever gone to someone's home where you couldn't find the front door? Perhaps it was on the side of the house or overgrown with bushes. In the same way that you have difficulty finding the entrance so does energy in general. There are also homes where the front door may be obviously placed on the front of the home, but there is no pathway to get there. The front door looks abandoned because the residents only use the backdoor.

Doors represent opportunities. And the front door is the primary door for opportunities. That is not to say that opportunities can't come in the through the backdoor. However, the backdoor is generally the way energy exits the home. Similar to our respiratory system, the front door is the inhale breath and the back door is the exhale breath. The front door brings in fresh air and exhales out old, processed air. This is essential for balance. It is therefore important to use the front door as much as possible even if you use the backdoor or garage door to enter and exit the home.

The front entrance of your home should be clearly delineated with house numbers, a doorbell or door knocker, and a welcome mat. This not only makes your front door obvious, but also welcoming. Also be aware of any trees, shrubs, or other foliage that may be blocking the energy coming in through your front door. This is especially important for selling a home. If the front door is not obviously visible, then potential buyers will not energetically see the house. Of course, they may be able to see it with their physical eyes, but the house will escape them energetically.

Front Entrance

The front entrance sets the tone for the entire home. In some homes, you might enter into grand foyer with tall ceilings up to the second story. Or the entrance could be a small, enclosed enclave. Can you see straight back to the backdoor? What is your view from the entrance? What rooms are visible? And where does the energy circulate to once you enter the home? All of these considerations will set the tone for the entire house similar to the way a first impression is set when you meet someone for the first time.

Once you enter the front door, you ideally walk into a foyer. Foyers are transitional spaces. The importance of adequate transitional spaces is often overlooked. They allow beneficial chi to rest and accumulate before moving into the next room. They set the stage for the bigger rooms, similar to an opening act. It only makes the main act that much more anticipated and better. I have recently seen new construction homes that eliminate a designated foyer in order to cut down on square footage. In homes without a foyer, you will immediate walk into a dining room or family room, which makes the energy too fast and rushing for those rooms. It will feel unsettling to eat, rest, or even focus in those rooms.

If you live in a space that does not have a designated foyer or entry space built in, then create one. One way is to place a rug just inside the door helping to separate the space just inside the door with the room you are entering. Another way is to hang a picture on one of the sidewalls as you enter the space. This will help the energy to rest in the entry before moving forward. In a former home, you enter right into a sitting room instead of a designated foyer. Like a foyer, the energy is able to accumulate in this room before moving into the family room. The low, lounge-like furniture helps to transition this area so that it doesn't rush into the family room. Had we decided to use the front room as the family room, it would have felt too unsettled being so close to the front door.

In another previous home, the entry led right into an open dining room space. While it was a beautiful dining room it rarely got used. Due to its location, it became a transitional space into the kitchen. Whatever room the front door (or backdoor if used as primary entrance) immediately opens into will become a transitional space even if not intended. If you enter into a kitchen, dining room, office, or family room, it will always have a transitional feel that is not quite settled as it otherwise would be.

Unfortunately, not all floor plans include an auspicious entry into a space. The most problematic entry is when you walk into the home and run right into a wall. This could lead to blocks or feeling blocked in your life. The wall immediately stops the beneficial chi from fully entering your home. It is important to open this area up energetically. If architecturally feasible, removing the wall or a section of the wall would be the first consideration. Another option is to place a mirror on the wall, which will help push the energy through the wall similar to a window or cut-out of the wall.

Another problematic entry is if you can see the backdoor straight back from the front door. This is similar to the shotgun-style house described in Chapter 3. However, other styles of homes have this arrangement. Like a shotgun, the energy enters through the front door only to have it rush out the backdoor. If you have ever had the front door and backdoor open at the same time and noticed how the airflow rushes through the home, this is indicative of how the energy flows in general with this floor plan. This same energy pattern can occur if the front door opens up to a long hallway. Even if there is not a backdoor lined up, the energy will immediately race down the hallway.

The best way to remedy this floor plan is to distract the energy, so to speak, from rushing out the backdoor. If there is a room of furniture between the front and backdoor this will inherently help to slow the energy down. However, if the pathway is more like a hallway or an open pathway, then it is best to attract the energy to the right and/or left of this pathway. You can use a mirror and/or interesting artwork to attract the energy toward a different direction. Hanging a crystal between the front and backdoor can also help distribute the energy more evenly.

A floor plan that creates confusing energy is the split-level home. Luckily this floor plan is considered outdated and hopefully will not return. All floor plan trends are an expression of the collective consciousness of a particular time period. When you enter the front door of a split-level home, you are immediately given a choice: upstairs or downstairs. Its occupants will always be faced with dilemmas, choices, and confusion. The overall energy in the home will be confusing. The homeowners of this floor plan usually resort to using the backdoor as the primary entrance instead. If you have a split-level floor plan, then give visual cues to which direction you want the energy to go, which is usually to the main level floor. Attract the energy either up or down the stairs with artwork, plants, or other décor items so that there is no decision to be made about which way to go upon entering.

Hallways

Hallways connect rooms like veins and arteries connect major organ systems throughout the body. Newer homes with an open floor plan and loft-style apartments have few, if any, hallways. Rooms connect without walls like lines blurred on a page. This allows for an openness of space and can be easier to breathe in. It can also blur the functions of rooms and make it difficult to know how to best use a function of a room. For example, a kitchen that opens up into a living room with no wall divider at all, can sometimes feel unsettling to those relaxing, or trying to relax, in the living room. At the same time, the person cooking feels connected to those in the living room.

Hallways are great for dividing spaces where necessary. For example, you may want the master bedroom to have more privacy from the public spaces, such as the living room or kitchen. A hallway can provide this space of division that is essential to a good night's sleep. At the same time, hallways should be used consciously and sparingly. Too many hallways can lead to too much division in the space, especially in the case of long hallways. Hallways can make the walls feel like they are coming in on their occupants and even affect breathing patterns within the home for its residents.

Have you ever been to a home where the rooms are grand with tall ceilings and then you walk into a tight hallway with a low ceiling? The transition is too quick and you suddenly feel like your breath has been cut off. The width, height, and length of hallways should be proportional to their adjoining rooms and used purposefully. You should also avoid having a bathroom at the end of a long hallway. All the energy rushes down the hallway and down the toilet. Keep the bathroom door closed at all times. In the case of a door, place a curtain over the window to avoid energy loss.

In the case of a hallway that feels too long or too dark, place a mirror on the side wall, have adequate lighting, and avoid placing furniture along the wall. Hanging a crystal from the ceiling is also a way to get the chi flowing properly as well. Hallways are iconical for displaying family photos. Be mindful not to hang so many that the hallway feels clogged up.

Stairways

As you will read in Chapter 10, stairways represent opportunities for growth and taking things to the next level. They are transitional spaces that connect us from one dimension to another. However they can also be jarring to the flow of a home if not placed correctly, creating too abrupt of a transition. How they are placed within a home can significantly shift the flow of energy.

Similar to a chute, the energy can rush up and down a staircase. For this reason, it is best that a staircase not be located in front of the front door. The energy rushes up the stairs as opposed to being distributed among the main level. It will also rush down the stairs and out the door. Having a staircase with a landing partly up the stairs helps alleviate a rush of energy up and down the staircase. Just as the landing is a resting spot for those climbing the stairs, it does the same for energy in general. Landings also serve to change the direction of energy, which slows the energy as well.

A staircase with the opening lined up with the front door creates a similar energy dynamic as when the backdoor is lined up with the front door. The remedy is similar too. You want to distract the energy from rushing upstairs by attracting it to the right or left sides. You can accomplish this by using a mirror or artwork to attract energy to rooms or hallways to the right or left of the staircase. You can also hang a crystal anywhere in the vicinity to more evenly distribute the energy.

Floor plans commonly place a stairway in the center of the home. It is important that the center of the home have a good flow of energy as it represents health according to the Bagua Map. In the case of a staircase in the center of the home, it is important that the energy circulate easily and freely around the staircase. Usually there is a circular pattern around the staircase made up of hallways and rooms. Be mindful that these areas flow unobstructed without furniture or clutter blocking the pathways with at least a three-foot walk-through space around this area. If this pathway does not circle around and instead comes to a dead-end wall, then place a mirror on that wall to help push the energy through completing this circle of energy.

It is advisable to avoid homes with a spiral staircase. While they may add functionality and a novelty to the space, they are detrimental to the health of the occupants. The energy up and down a spiral staircase is hard, abrasive, sudden, and similar to that of a corkscrew drilling down into your home. Aside from health concerns, the section of the Bagua Map in which the spiral staircase is located will experience challenges as well. If architecturally feasible, it is best to remove the spiral staircase altogether. If that is not possible, then hang a crystal above or as close to above the staircase as possible. Place a plant at the top and/or bottom of the staircase to soften the energy and ground the energy better.

Bathrooms

Early homes had it right: the bathroom goes outside in an outhouse. Unfortunately, there is no good place for a bathroom with regard to feng shui. Due to the drains and flushing in a bathroom, the energy exits the home in the same draining and flushing manner. The phrases, "money going down the drain" or "your love life down the tubes" are common in our language. These precisely describe the energy of toilets and drains, which is why they can disrupt the energy in a home.

In feng shui, water is energetically considered the same as money. In bathrooms, all the water is flushing out of the home and therefore money is as well. In scientific terms, energy attracts to water and will therefore exit down the toilet and down drains. Think of lightning being attracted to water. Lightning is simply a concentrated form of energy.

Water is also representative of emotions, which makes a bathroom in the Love section particularly toxic as well. Clearly we can't live without a bathroom, but there are some locations better than others as discussed below. The bathroom is least desirable and should be avoided, if possible, in the Wealth, Fame, Love, and Health sectors.

Bathroom in Wealth Corner- In working with clients, I have found a strong correlation between those with money issues and their bathroom being located in the Wealth Corner (back left corner of your home). This is consistent with traditional feng shui rules. I have witnessed many floor plans with this arrangement, most of which were experiencing financial problems.

I have seen clients who, as soon as they move into a house with the bathroom in the Wealth Corner, suddenly lose their job, get laid off, or have to take a job making less money. Another common scenario is that while their income stays the same, their expenses go up. In other words, the money is incoming and equally outgoing to where it seems like the money is "going down the drain."

I have also been in many homes with this arrangement where the occupants experienced no financial difficulties. That is possible as well. Nevertheless, it's best to avoid a floor plan with the bathroom in the Wealth Corner. Who knows, even those who didn't have any financial maladies may have also missed out on more prosperity or simply had more peace of mind or less stress in managing their money with a different bathroom arrangement.

The bathroom should also be avoided in the Fame Section of the Bagua Map as well. The energy of Fame & Reputation usually coincides directly with one's income and wealth. It is rare to have a bad reputation and have a generous flow of income. In fact, usually the fame or reputation comes first before the money starts flowing in. Furthermore, the Fame section of the Bagua Map holds the energy of the Fire Element. The watery nature of bathrooms will put the fire out in this section of the home. In addition to the suggested remedies for bathrooms, add accents of red to the bathroom to help bring the fire element back into this section. Add candles as well.

Bathroom in Love Corner- Having a bathroom in the Love Corner can make relationships challenging, or at least, emotional. I had one client with a bathroom in the Love Corner in the home they built and raised their family. While they appeared to have a happy and functional marriage, the underpinnings of their current problem were taking place over those 15 years. A feng shui remedy may show immediate changes that are considered positive, or it may speed up the inevitable end of a relationship. Keep in mind that it is never the home to blame for the problems as there is always a vibrational match to moving into a house with a particular floor plan from the beginning. This is why becoming more conscious of feng shui principles can lead to a more conscious lifestyle overall.

Bathroom Inside Kitchen- The energy of a kitchen is the complete opposite to that of a bathroom. The kitchen is about taking in nourishment while the bathroom is about excreting waste. It is best not to mix these two functions by placing a bathroom door opening up from the kitchen. This could lead to digestive or other imbalances within the home. In the event of this floor plan configuration, it is best to keep the door closed to the bathroom at all times.

Bathroom in Center of Home- Due to the downward energy that comes with a bathroom it is best not to have a bathroom in the center of the home. It is important that the center of the home have auspicious energy flowing throughout as it represents the health or overall wellbeing for the household. Having a bathroom in the center can cause instability with health, wealth, and overall harmony in the home. To counteract the downward energy of the bathroom's water elements, it is best to help ground the space. To do so, you can add a heavy piece of furniture, such as a heavy sink table or add stone or pottery décor. Placing a rock or gemstone in each of the four corners is another way to help ground in the space.

Bathroom Near Front Door Entry- Another undesirable location for a bathroom is near the front door. This could include a powder room adjacent to the entry, a bathroom that can be seen from the entry, or even a bathroom above the foyer entry. As the primary chi enters the home, the last thing you want is for it to go right down the toilet.

For bathrooms visible from the entry, it is best to keep the door closed at all times, along with the other remedies suggested for bathrooms. Rooms located below a bathroom can also experience negative effects. For example, if a bathroom is located over an entry, it can disrupt the chi as it enters the home. If a bathroom is located above a bedroom, this can be unsettling and even lead to illness.

Best Placement for Bathroom- Bathrooms are best placed in the Creativity and Family sections of the Bagua Map. Both of these sections are compatible with Water elements and are not as susceptible to financial loss. The Helpful People & Travel and Wisdom & Knowledge sections are also compatible so long as these sections of the floor plan are not visible from the front door.

5 Remedies for an Inauspiciously-Located Bathroom

If you already live in a home in one of the challenging areas discussed, then it is best to use one or more of the following feng shui remedies:

1. **Keep the toilet lid closed.** This is easy and usually a crowd favorite among women.
2. **Close drains.** Keep the drains closed when not in use.
3. **Red ribbon.** Tie a red ribbon around the plumbing pipes coming in and out of the sink and toilet. This is a remedy used in Black Hat Feng Shui methodology. The ribbon is preferably 9" long and doesn't need to be seen. The color red neutralizes the negative draining energy.

4. **Earth Elements.** Use Earth elements to contain the Water elements by decorating with baskets, potted plants, pottery, and rocks.

5. **Renovation.** This is a drastic remedy and should be done only as a last resort. While you can relocate a bathroom to a more auspicious location, don't be surprised if energy gets stirred up soon thereafter. Moving fixtures can disrupt the energy in a home until relocated and grounded in.

6. **Feng shui mirror.** Place a feng shui mirror, octagon-shaped beveled mirror, on the outside of the door threshold going into the bathroom. This reflects the energy out of the bathroom preventing it from entering the bathroom at all. This remedy should be used sparingly as it works similar to amputation. It is best to try to save the limb first before cutting it off.

7. **Love Your Bathroom.** Enjoying the rooms in your home is the best feng shui remedy. This includes your bathroom. Decorate your bedroom as you would any room to make it a room you love to be in.

Garage

The amount of space garages occupy in a home continues to increase with each decade. In my historical neighborhood, there are no original attached garages as cars were not as common as they are today. In the 1960's and 70's detached garages were incorporated into floor plans. In our present day, houses are rarely designed without a garage. While they serve a functional purpose, they can also disrupt the energy in the home.

Garages are for the purpose of storing your car, but they usually double as storage for tools, supplies, and recreation equipment. Most garages become a haven for clutter. Items that are to be given away end up in the garage, as well as items that the homeowners don't know what else to do with. Unfortunately, this is all negative energy that is contained within the home. Even without the clutter, the energy of cars moving in and out of the home can be unsettling, particularly to rooms adjacent or above the garage. For this reason, it is best not to have a bedroom placed over the garage.

When placing the Bagua Map over the floor plan, the garage is included. Garages are often located on the back of the house in the Wealth or Love Corners. When my clients or workshop participants find out that their Love is in the garage, they usually respond with "Well, that explains it!"

When garages are found on the front of the house, it is representative of a focus on their cars. Cars symbolize status, career, and direction in life. Garages on the front of a house usually end up creating an imbalanced L-shaped home as opposed to a more auspicious square or rectangle home. The garage either creates a missing corner or becomes an extension for the overall footprint of the home. Either way, it is best to treat the garage just like any other room in the house. Avoid storing clutter. Keep it organized. You could even paint the walls and add a picture or two.

Being aware of where these particular rooms and areas fall on the floor plan is important considerations when purchasing a home. While no floor plan is perfect, knowledge is power. And where your floor plan is challenged, you can make appropriate adjustments. The shape of the house, floor plan, and physical characteristics of a home are evident, the energy of a space may not always be. As we move into the next chapters, we'll go deeper into the energetics of a space starting with the energy left behind by the previous owners.

CHAPTER 5

YOUR HOME'S PAST - PREVIOUS OWNERS

> *[W]e must begin by understanding that every place is given its character by certain patterns of events that keep on happening there.*
>
> —The Timeless Way of Building.

We all enter into relationships with a history, a past, and maybe even some old baggage. Your home is no different. Your home has a past too with as many past relationships as its past owners and occupants. One of the most underestimated energies that affect homeowners is the energy left by previous owners, also referred to as *predecessor energy*. Did the previous owners file bankruptcy, get a divorce, or fall ill? Was the home foreclosed upon? Was there a pattern of occupants suddenly getting transferred out of state? Was there trauma that took place in the home? These are all questions that are important to know, if possible, before moving into a space.

My client, Wendy, called me about six months into moving into their home. After a series of unexplainable and unfortunate incidents, she and her husband were considering putting the house back on the market. It started the day they moved in when a neighbor came by and mentioned that the previous owner had committed suicide in the home. She further told them that there had been a relative living in the basement with mental problems and she suspected he was involved in unscrupulous activity. Although she was spooked a bit, Wendy didn't think too much of it until their two-year old Lab developed an unexplainable brain tumor. It wasn't much longer thereafter that the couple began experiencing strange accidents around the home followed by financial problems.

Upon arriving at the home, the first thing I noticed was the lot on which the house sat. There was a drainage ditch on the side of the property draining down a hill. While you don't want overflow rainwater draining toward your home, you also don't want the neighborhood's water draining on your property either. The house was also sitting at an odd-angled corner lot incongruent to the neighborhood. Although seemingly unrelated to someone committing suicide in a home, the fact is negative energy attracts negative energy. Usually when there is negative energy it will start to domino into more negative energy. And it usually starts with the land as discussed in Chapter 1.

When it came time to space clear the home, I was intuitively led to the area where the suicide took place and cleared the energy around that trauma. When I went downstairs to clear the other trauma in the basement I was stopped in my tracks. Every hair on my arm was raised and I felt a strong aversion from going further. Wendy had avoided going into the basement and had not been down there since moving in. In fact, it was clear that they had just dumped their clutter and unpacked boxes in the space with the hopes of not having to ever go back downstairs. This was another example of negative energy attracting more negative energy. Usually in areas where trauma has occurred, there will be an accumulation of clutter in the same area.

Laced in my energetic protective bubbles, stones, and mantras, I continued on. After an arduous hour, I was able to clear the energy from the basement as much as possible. I encouraged my client to declutter the space and proceed with renovating the space. The more the owners energetically "own" the space going forward, the more it will help to continue transforming the energy. Luckily, this couple had the knowledge to have the space cleared before experiencing more negativity or selling the home to the next unlucky buyer. While this was an extreme example, it shows just how much the energy of previous owners can have on the energy of a home and our lives. It is important to learn the history of your home prior to purchasing it, especially that of the most recent owners.

Patterns of Energy

Our home is the space in which we are the most vulnerable and emotional. We are continually emitting our emotions through our energy field throughout our day. We often use the phrase, "what happens behind closed doors," meaning we do things in our private home that we would not do anywhere else. Our home is the container for our emotions. As our emotions are emitted into a space it can affect the energy field of other occupants. Energy is actually absorbed into the walls, and even taken on by the furniture, floors, and furnishings.

The heavier and denser the energy the more likely it is to coagulate or stagnate in parts, places, and crevices of your home. From a scientific perspective, the higher the energy vibration of energy, the lighter the energy. We often refer to this as "good" or "positive" energy. By its very essence, the higher the vibration of energy, the less likely it will become stagnant. On the other hand, a slow frequency or low vibration is heavy and dense and more prone to stagnation. We think of this as "bad" or "negative" energy. Regardless, like attracts like and over time the same vibration will attract more and more of the same type of energy. Eventually, as a result, patterns get created.

Think about the last time you went on a long vacation. While on vacation we start to take on different routines and habits. We start expanding our mind and perspectives. You might have even declared you would make some lifestyle changes upon returning home, such as a new exercise program or healthier eating. However, within hours of returning home you simply fall back into your same patterns. Your patterns are within your home. Partially, this is due to the location, floor plan, and other factors discussed in preceding chapters, but it is also because of energy patterns in your home that may have started with previous owners, and definitely patterns carried forth in day-to-day living.

In *The Timeless Way of Building*, Alexander focuses on the power of patterns in our world, our lives, and our living spaces. In fact, this idea of patterns was such a prevalent theme that it spawned his next book and classic, *Pattern Language*. Alexander theorizes that our world has a structure that is made up of repeated patterns that largely accounts for the events that take place. He says that we "tend to forget too easily that all the life and soul of a place, all of our experiences that, depend not simply on the physical environment, but on the patterns of events which we experience there."[4]

These patterns are ingrained within our cultures, our families, and individual lives. Our living spaces are the holder of these patterns and largely determine our daily life while living there.

> "Activities; events; forces; situations; lightning strikes; fish die; water flows; lovers quarrel; a cake burns; cats chase each other; a hummingbird sits outside my window; friends come by; my car breaks down; lovers' reunion; children born; grandparents broke…
>
> My life is made of episodes like this.
>
> The life of every person, animal, plant, creature, is made of similar episodes.
>
> The character of a place, then, is given to it by the episodes which happen there."[5]

---

[4] A Timeless Way of Building, p. 62.
[5] A Timeless Way of Building, p. 62.

Patterns in our spaces are created by repetition that locks in the energy, specifically in the water molecules, and keeps those in its grip stuck as well. As a result, we are prevented from making changes. This is why it is important to space clear your home upon or before moving in. Even if there were no negative or traumatic events in a home's history, it is still imperative to space clear before moving into a space. You do not want to fall into the patterns of those who previously lived in the space. Instead, create your own conscious energy, choices, and memories.

Foreclosed Homes

An emerging negative pattern in homes is foreclosures. The financial collapse of 2008 left many with financial woes. It also took a particular beating on homes. Since 2008, a record number of homes have been foreclosed upon. According to RealtyTrac,[6] close to 3 million properties were foreclosed on just in 2010. A foreclosed home is usually accompanied with a decline in maintenance of the home. Repairs go undone, the yard is no longer adequately maintained, and improvements are certainly not made. It is common for occupants to simply leave the home in a cluttered, abandoned state upon being evicted. This alone wreaks havoc on the energy of a space. The homeowners may also hold resentment, remorse, or guilt toward the house itself.

Furthermore, the occupants undergo a high level of emotional stress, which is often accompanied by relationship stress within the home. While many theorize a correlation between foreclosure and divorce rates, the statistics are mixed. It would stand to reason that relationships are strained under such conditions since money is the number one reason for divorces. At the same time, many couples wanting divorce simply couldn't afford it. Because the real estate market was so bad, they couldn't afford to sell their home and instead forced to continue living together. In the case of a divorce, the potentially

---

[6] http://www.realtytrac.com/content/press-releases/record-29-million-us-properties-receive-foreclosure-filings-in-2010-despite-30-month-low-in-december-6309

foreclosed home may even become a pawn or bargaining tool, a far cry from the white picket fenced American dream the homeowners may have had upon moving in.

When a new owner moves in, the home is layered with the energy of the distraught, foreclosed, previous owners. Without a proper and deep clearing of the previous owners' energy, the new owners will most likely struggle in this new home. One of my clients, Denise, and her husband purchased a foreclosed condo. When they took ownership, the home was trashed. According to neighbors, the previous owner was extremely messy and most likely a hoarder. At the time, however, the price was too good for them to turn down and they were eager to make it work.

From the moment Denise moved in, she did not like being in the space. She said that whatever she did to the space it never felt like home. She even found reasons not to go home at times. It was in their second year of living there when they began experiencing financial challenges and soon thereafter marital problems. By the end of the second year, they filed for divorce. It turned out that instead of fighting over who kept the home, they fought over who had to keep it.

It's important to be consciously aware of the energy in your home and not fall into a negative energy pattern that is not even yours. Although we are energetically attracted to homes that are a "match" for us, there is no reason to enhance a negative energy pattern already within ourselves if it can be avoided. If you already live in a space with a negative past, then it is imperative to hire a feng shui consultant or energy healer to clear the space. Space clearing techniques can be performed by the homeowners as prescribed in this book. However, it is sometimes advisable to have someone outside the household perform the clearing in such cases where the occupants' energy is too closely intertwined with the negative energy that needs to be cleared.

In the case of Denise and her husband who bought the foreclosed home, it's not coincidental that the couple found a home in such bad straits. Although their relationship did not show visible signs of having problems at the time they purchased the condo, underneath the surface their relationship was fragile and they were therefore a vibrational match to the space. While divorce or financial difficulty may not be avoided regardless of where you live, living in a positive energetic environment can help bring an amicable transition or resolution. It turned out that the couple's divorce turned quite nasty, not too unlike the state of the condo when they moved in.

Ghosts and Other Entities

I never sought out to be a ghost buster, but I soon learned that it was part of the job description for a feng shui consultant. Perhaps not coincidentally, I grew up in a neighborhood that had many reports of ghost activity. The home I grew up in sat on what was believed to be former Native American grounds. In fact, the neighborhood was named Indian Lake Forest for this reason. On the adjacent empty lot was a cave where we would find arrowheads as frequently as we would snakes and crawdads. My best friend lived across the street and for about five years, her home and the adjacent home experienced occurrences consistent with ghost activity.

The oven would mysteriously turn on. The dog would suspiciously start barking in the middle of night at something across the room. Items would go missing. Even the realtor showing the adjacent house experienced an incident that was to never bring her back to the house again. It was theorized among the residents that it was a Native American that had once lived on the land. Despite having spent a lot of time at my best friend's home, I was never scared of the prospect of a ghost and although the stories were interesting, I was unattached to the drama around it. I now see how this is an important component to successfully clearing spaces.

There are a lot of theories relating to whether ghosts really exist. Most people have experienced some sort of paranormal occurrence in a space to give them reason to believe in ghosts or some sort of entity. People often report a presence in a room, someone touching them, unexplained noises, footsteps when no one else is at home, among many other common occurrences.

One theory is that a ghost is just a ball of leftover energy that builds and becomes more sophisticated over time. Others theorize that souls become trapped in between dimensions, similar to that depicted in the movie *Ghost*. Regardless of one's belief the commonality in most incidences of paranormal activity is that the energy can be pinpointed to a specific room or area of the house. Particularly in the event of a traumatic event, the energy will become trapped in that particular area of the house and become reinforced over years, each time someone re-experiences the ghost-like activity. The thought form or ghost can be as sophisticated as an apparition or as faint as a slight feeling you get as you walk into a room.

The more severe the trauma, the denser the energy will be and the more likely it will get stuck. Years or even centuries later, a sensitive person may pick up on the energy. There is usually something within them that resonates with the energy. Each time someone reacts to the negative energy, whether conscious of why or not, it grows and become more and more sophisticated. For occupants not sensitive to the energy, they too will be affected by the negative energy on some level, but not be as aware of it.

Ghost activity is an extreme case of what happens everyday within our homes. Suppose your spouse or teenage son comes home after a bad day. An argument ensues in the living room. As the energy is released from the argument, those emotions will hang out in that area of the home. Whether they dissipate will depend on the severity of the emotions and also the feng shui of the room. As the emotions linger in the space, it becomes more likely for an argument to break out in the same place in the near future.

This same concept pertains to other types of situations besides arguments. For example, there was a spot in the kitchen where my former chocolate lab was afraid to go into because the floor transitioned from carpet to tile. In this area is a cabinet with pantry items. Not coincidentally, items are commonly dropped in the same location. Our dog's constant skittishness in this area leaves an unsettled energy leading to accidents such as these. Positive energy can also be instilled into a space as well. Think of your favorite spot in your home. It most likely holds only positive associations for you. The same is the case with a meditation space. As the meditative energy builds over time, it makes it easier each time to drop into meditation.

Sometimes the energy of just one person is enough to leave a trail of negative energy for others. You've most likely walked into someone's home, individual room, or office only to want to just turn right back around and leave. They may be a highly negative person in general or depressed or extremely angry. The energy around people involved in drug activity or illegal activity will leave a dark energy in their immediate surroundings. When you visit a prospective space, be conscious of how you feel walking in each room. Your intuition is your best guide as to the energy of a space.

Ghost Busting

Ghost busting is a more in-depth form of space clearing. Some forms of energy are a little more stubborn than others. What I have found in my experience in clearing ghosts is that it is never coincidental that the ghost and the homeowners are attracted to one another. In other words, moving into a "haunted" house or acquiring a ghost while living somewhere is not about bad luck or coincidence. There is a reason, or a resonance, between the ghost energy and that of its occupants.

For example, one of the first homes I cleared with a ghost was that of Carol, a single mom. After a year or two of living in their home, strange occurrences began happening. They would hear random noises in the attic. Below that area was the kitchen where they kept experiencing problems with the lighting and mechanicals. Carol, being intuitive herself, would occasionally feel a presence that she picked up as a little girl. It was in her bedroom, which was also located above the kitchen. She commented how her house was very welcoming and how she loved having the neighborhood kids and as many people as possible in her home. It was in this same conversation when she mentioned that she missed having more children around as her daughter was getting older. This was a clue to the resonant energy between the ghost and my client.

I space cleared the home without detecting anything out of the ordinary until I came to Carol's bedroom. The hair on my arms stood straight up and my hands felt like I was petting a purring cat. As I continued feeling around the bedroom, I was led to an area near the bed. Strangely enough, there was an antique baby carriage sitting next to the bed with blankets and pillows piled on top although the rest of the bedroom was neat and orderly.

My hands were buzzing. I lifted the blankets off the carriage and was startled to see an old doll staring me in the face. I knew I had found the ghost. Ghosts or entities will often find an object or objects through which to manifest into our 3D world. Faces in pictures, sculptures, or dolls can be a common venue through which an entity may express itself. That being said, any area without adequate lighting, lots of clutter, little movement, or a location with stagnant energy and/or bad feng shui will be an inviting location for a ghost-like energy.

I asked Carol about the baby carriage and doll and she said it was a family piece. She too wasn't sure why she had kept it in her bedroom. Upon my suggestions, she began to realize that she was experiencing the beginnings of empty nest syndrome -- longing to have small children in the house. The ghost in the form of a little girl was filling this void. We moved the carriage and I space cleared the area. She agreed to move the carriage and doll out of the home for good and to more consciously deal with the reality of her daughter growing up.

Sometimes it's possible that the reason why a ghost presents itself in your space is so that you will free it. It is a common belief that some ghosts are stuck souls with unfinished business that needs to be taken care of before they are able to fully release themselves from this dimension and move on. I believe this was the case in a home where I once lived. Within a few weeks of living there, one night I was relaxing on the couch and glared off into the dining room when I saw an apparition of a cross and skull bones clear as day.

I was quite startled as this was the first time I had ever seen anything resembling an apparition, let alone in the form of a skull and crossbones. I tried to discount my vision, but I couldn't help but remember that the home was used as a parishioner's house in the early 1900's. It was during the night when I got my answers through a dream. In the dream, I witnessed the entire story as if it were a movie. The ghost, when living, had been involved in some sort of illegal activity. He had come to the preacher's home for forgiveness and never received it.

It was October 30 and a blustery evening when I released the ghost. It was an intuitive clearing that I did through a meditation in the area I had seen the apparition. I knew the goal would be to help this stuck soul get the forgiveness he needed. While I am not equipped to deliver forgiveness as a preacher would, I did my best and then showed him a higher vibration of love and light. He accepted this and transitioned into a higher dimension.

What was most interesting was the feeling that overtook me. For a split moment, I could feel that higher dimension of white light and soaked in it until brought back down to Earth. But what was the most surprising was the sudden emptiness I felt in the space. This was also followed by a momentary emptiness within myself. I would have never thought of myself as wanting the company of ghosts, but for a split second I understood how their energy fills a space and a void in people's lives if not aware of it.

I realized that his energy had been taking up my own energy. When we let others - real people or ghosts - cross boundaries and take up our energetic space, we are allowing them to take our power as well. The previous owner was an old man that had lived there for about 30 years apparently feeling at home with this ghost, and vice versa. However, when I moved in, it was clear that we both could not coexist in the house. I believe the cross and skull bones apparition was to get my attention to free him once and for all.

But My Ghost is Friendly!

Until my personal experience with this ghost, I never imagined that people might want to keep their ghost around. However, this is a scenario I run into quite often with clients. They are aware that they have a ghost, but do not want it cleared. For example, I had one client that lived in a stately home with a rich history in a historical neighborhood. There is a female ghost that several different family members have seen around the house. When seen, she is tending to the house as if she is still caring for the home. When my client mentioned the presence of the ghost, I asked if she would like for me to clear it. She was adamant that I not clear it. She said, "You can clear anything, but not my ghost!" She was comforted, feeling the presence of a female woman taking care of the home. She felt like the ghost was a positive energy and should be kept with the house.

I have now learned to get the consent from clients when they want me to clear a ghost. Even if they hire me to specifically clear a ghost or other entity, I find it helpful to have them affirmatively state that they are ready for the energy to be cleared. They are often surprised at themselves when they have to pause and think about it and the consequences. Like a codependent relationship, the energy has been serving them on some level.

Space Clearing

By now, you are hopefully wondering how to space clear your home. Space clearing has been used by many different cultures for hundreds, if not thousands, of years. Different cultures use different methods in accordance with their traditions, but some of the more common methods are described below.

Sage Smudging- Using a sage stick, also known as a smudge stick, is a tradition borrowed from Native Americans and now used worldwide as a space clearing technique. A smudge stick consists of a bundle of herbs. Sage is usually the primary herb and often mixed with other herbs such as lavender, cedar, and sweetgrass. Smudge sticks are usually available in natural health food stores, metaphysical shops, and online. Anyone sensitive to smoke or who finds the scent of burning sage unpleasant, can opt for using a smudge spray. I have formulated a Smudge Spray that is hand-blended and can be used in lieu of burning sage.

Sound- Using sound is another effective space clearing technique and can be performed using bells, singing bowls, chimes, drums, tuning forks, and even clapping. Sound creates a harmonic resonance throughout the entire space. The sound will ripple throughout the space and beyond long after our human ears can actually hear the sound. Sound produces an immediate vibrational shift in the room and can also be a conduit for sacred geometry. Music is a form of geometry with certain notes and combination of notes considered sacred.

Bells are the most common sound method for space clearing. It is best to use bells made from base metals, such as brass, silver, copper, lead, or tin to activate a yang (active) energy. If you have multiple bells, then start with the largest, or deepest, bell working your way to the smaller, higher-pitched bells that fine-tune the energy. Using sound not only clears the space, but also helps to revitalize and reenergize your home.

Salts- Another common method for space clearing is using salt. Salt naturally extracts negative energy. It has been used for its healing powers for thousands of years and even used as currency in Ancient China. Have you ever had an injury or wound and swam in the ocean? By the end of the day, you were miraculously healed. We replicate this naturally healing tonic by taking Epson salt baths.

Just as we use salt to extract negative energy from our body, it can also be used to extract negative energy from our spaces. To do so, have a bowl of salt and set your intention. You can use table salt or sea salt. Sprinkle or toss pinches of salt into all four corners of a room. Set the remaining bowl of salt in the center of the room. Allow the salt to remain in the space overnight. The next day you can remove the salt and invoke the space with intentions of positive energy.

Healing professionals often keep a bowl of salt in their space for the purpose of keeping the energy neutralized in their healing space. This is why you will often see Himalayan salt lamps used in healing spaces as well. Salt has also been used in clearing negative entities and ghosts. A bowl of salt is placed in the location of the disturbance and near an open window. This is said to allow the energy to escape the space.

Once you have chosen your space clearing modality, you can begin your space clearing session with the following steps adapted from Denise Linn's book, *Sacred Space*.

Steps for Space Clearing[7]

1. *Preparation-* Make sure your own energy is in check. Do not space clear if you are sick or your energy is not at its best. It is also best if the space has been physically cleaned and/or clutter picked up.

2. *Set an Intention-* Any time you space clear you should have a purpose or intention in mind before starting. In the case of addressing a specific issue, then your purpose or intention should be obvious. For example, your intention may be to "clear away negative emotions from my ex-boyfriend" or "clear out stagnant energy and enhance a positive energy flow to attract prospective buyers."

3. *Clear the Space-* Using your chosen modality, start at the front door of the space. Work around the perimeter of the space first, going room by room. Be particularly mindful of corners, dark spaces, and behind furniture. One rule of thumb is that where dirt and cobwebs lurk, so does stagnant energy.

---

[7] These steps for space clearing are inspired from Linn, Denise, *Space Clearing: Clearing and Enhancing the Energy of Your Home* (Wellspring/Ballantine 2007).

4. *Invoke the Space-* After you have cleared the space, it is important to invoke the space with a positive energy. This can be done for the entire space or room by room. For example, the overall intention for the home could be "for harmonic relationships" or "light and love" or "for the right buyer." For individual rooms, such as the kitchen, it could be "to enjoy healthy meals with my family." Seal in the invocation by burning a candle or incense, saying a prayer or mantra, or any other dedication to help seal in your invocation.

How Often Should You Space Clear?

I advise giving your home periodic space clearings. This helps maintain a positive energy flow throughout the space. Think of it as preventative medicine for your home. For myself, anytime that I give the home a thorough cleaning, I will follow it up with a space clearing. I also space clear anytime the energy feels stagnant. Once you tune into your home's energy, you will become more intuitive about when it needs clearing. Here are some examples of when you might space clear for general maintenance:

- After clearing clutter
- Starting a new program or positive habit
- After sickness in the home
- You received bodywork yourself and want your home to also have a renewed state of well-being.
- After cleaning your home
- General fatigue
- Coming home from vacation
- Spring cleaning
- At the New Year to invoke positive new energy

Even if you are space clearing for general maintenance, it is still important to set an intention while space clearing. For example, "to create a positive energy flow" or "to have a fresh start for the month." Once you have finished space clearing, look around the room. You will notice that the room looks crisper and colors are brighter. Also notice your breath. You will be able to breathe more deeply. Feel your body. You will feel much lighter. You will feel immediate benefits from clearing your home that will positively affect your health and well-being.

CHAPTER 6

OUR ENERGY, OUR EMOTIONS, AND OUR STUFF

Your living space is such a powerful metaphor because everything in it--every pot, plant, and pillow--reflects choices we make from among countless options, for countless reasons. The portrait that emerges is all the more accurate for having been created unconsciously.

—Martha Beck

Remember the last time you moved into a new home. Within minutes, the quiet space turned into an energy soup of chaos with boxes, furniture, and a boatload of emotions. We quickly begin filling in the space with our furniture, décor items, artwork, storage, dishes, memorabilia, and collectibles. We also fill the space with our own personal energy. Not only do we bring our physical baggage, but our emotional baggage into the space as well.

Beyond the walls of the floor plan, we further divide the energy in a space by placing furniture around the house. Furniture directs the energy in new ways, which directly affects us – physically, mentally, and emotionally. And then there is our stuff – the dishes, clothing, and jewelry with our energetic imprinted upon them. The quilt from Aunt Sylvia, the vacation albums, the armoire you inherited, your favorite books, and so on. Our stuff holds our emotions and further affects the energy in spaces.

Feng shui, green design, and other environmental sciences provide us with important tools for utilizing and harmonizing the Earth's energy into our home. But the energy *we* bring into our home is underestimated and overlooked. The human mind is one of the most sophisticated and powerful instruments of energy known on Earth and has a profound impact on our immediate environment. Our energy field, which includes all of our thoughts, intentions, emotions, physical health, along with our past and present, affects our space. To further understand this unseen world of energy in our home, let's first take a look at how energy fields work.

Energy or Aura Fields

We've all had one of those days when nothing is going right. As you rush to get to work, you spill coffee all over your shirt. In frustration, you blame your dog by raising your voice as he drops his tail between his legs. Then while impatiently sitting in traffic, you call into work to let the receptionist know that you are running late just as your cell phone drops the call. To top it off, when you finally get into the office and turn your computer on, an error message comes up when you try to log in. Are all these problems coincidental? Of course not. Each incident affects the next as the negative energy builds and builds. Not only are you negatively affected, but so are your dog, the receptionist, your cellphone, and even your computer.

Because most people cannot actually see energy, we underestimate its impact on other people, objects, and our environment. We now know as the result of major advances in the science of quantum physics that everything, living or not living, is simply a composition of energy. Nothing is solid. A brick is actually a mass of vibrating atoms with the space between each atom equal to the space between each star in the Milky Way. Everything in your house, from your kitchen table to kitchen plumbing is made up of vibrating energy.

Although I had accepted this concept as scientific truth, I didn't fully grasp it until one rainy Saturday morning when I didn't want to get out of bed. I was gazing off out the window daydreaming about either the meaning of life or what I was going to have for lunch. That's when I noticed a glow around the curtain rod. I was seeing the curtain rod's energy field. I looked around the room with the same lazy gaze and could see energy fields around anything and everything in the room.[8] This moment completely revolutionized my feng shui work. Until then, I had only seen aura fields around people and plants. But this curtain rod had its own world going on. It emits and takes on energy as do plants, animals, and people.

People, animals, plants, and all objects are made up of vibrating energy, as is everything in our solar system and the universe itself. This vibration extends beyond the physical body or tangible object and is referred to as an energy, or aura, field. Think about a loud bass stereo speaker or a bright light bulb. You can feel the vibration beyond the actual speaker and see the light beyond the bulb. The same is true for energy fields. Although they are not as readily visible or heard at the frequency that most of us can see or hear, they are nonetheless very real.

The human energy field extends from six inches to three feet beyond the physical body. Thoughts and emotions swirl around the human aura field producing different colors visible with Kirlian photography. For example, an angry person will have bursts of red coming from around their head, while someone feeling very loving may have pink or green in their aura field. Because objects are not conscious beings with thoughts and emotions, their aura fields are not so changeable. The energy field of an inanimate object is determined by its physical composition and color. Plants, animals, and other living things have

---

[8] The best way to see aura fields is to relax the eyes and gaze beyond the person or object. While everything has an energy field, the more "alive" something is, the higher its frequency and easier to see its energy field.

more complex and changing aura fields depending on their level of consciousness.

Although most people do not see or tangibly feel energy fields, we have all detected them at some point without even realizing it. For example, your loved one walks into the house from work. The room is instantly tense or light depending on what kind of day he or she has had. Or perhaps you feel drained just being around a particular person. Another example is when someone stands in your personal space making you feel uncomfortable. That person is actually encroaching upon your energy field. We can also detect someone in the room or coming up behind us without actually seeing or hearing them.

Energy is often characterized in terms of being tangible, such as with the phrase, "You could cut the tension with a knife." All of these are instances in which we can detect energy beyond our five senses. In fact, we pick up on the energy through our aura field before our five senses ever do. One or more of our five senses then communicate the message to us. Although energy is not visible to most people, it is very real. We also don't see radio waves, but listen to the radio. We can't see electricity, but continue to plug in. And we can't see microwaves, but our soup explodes nevertheless when cooked too long.

When we think of being *energy conscious*, we normally don't think of it with regard to ourselves, but we should. Being conscious of our energy or thoughts is often referred to as using intention or being intentional. Everything in our physical surroundings is a manifestation of our minds and can be physically seen in form, such as a new car, a business, or a cup of coffee.

We can also consciously manifest on an energetic level. For example, if we want to cheer someone up, we might consciously say something funny. As a result, there will most likely be an energetic shift in the other person and in the entire room. Taking it a step further, you decide to send love to your mother by energetically sending her loving thoughts. Ten minutes later she calls you just because she was thinking about you. Of course, in the same way we can affect others positively, we can affect others negatively.

We are very powerful beings with the ability to consciously and unconsciously shift, or transform, energy. Thirty years ago, we would have found incredulous the idea of transacting business, buying stock, and Christmas shopping just by pressing a few buttons on a computer. The same is now true with the power of the mind. We are now living at a time when we can have profound and powerful effects on ourselves, others, and spaces with the power of the conscious mind by just sitting still and using our energy.

The human energy field is an exact blueprint of the physical, mental, emotional, and spiritual body, but in the form of energy. For example, during surgery, if an incision is made on the physical body, there is also an incision in the energy field. Current emotions and thoughts, along with any unreleased past emotions and memories, are also part of our energy field.

The Chakras

The human energy field can further be divided into seven energy centers, called the *chakras*. The energy we draw up from the Earth is processed or metabolized through the chakras. A chakra is an energy center that receives, processes, and expresses life force energy. The word *chakra* literally translates as *wheel* or *disk* in the Sanskrit language and describes the vortex of energy centers located in the human energy field. There are seven primary chakras that directly connect the physical body with the energy body. This connection is made via the endocrine system and is the basis for the mind body connection between the physical, emotional, and mental bodies. In other words, the chakras are the energetic bridge between the mind and body.

The seven chakras are the main portals through which we receive and metabolize energy. There is also a vast network of minor chakra points throughout the body as well, similar to the hundreds of meridian points used in acupuncture as part of Chinese Medicine. Although chakras are not visible to most people, they can energetically be felt, seen, and scientifically documented by many. The chakras emanate up from the physical body reaching out into the aura field as a spinning vortex connecting our internal and external worlds. Listed below are the seven major chakras with their correlating Sanskrit name and how they affect the energy in the body:

1st Chakra (Muladhara)- The 1st chakra is often referred to as the *root chakra*. It relates to our primal security and survival needs, such as food, shelter, and clothing. This chakra is located at the base of the tailbone and affects the low back, legs, and feet. It is our grounding force that connects us with Mother Earth. If this chakra is out of balance, it can lead to feeling ungrounded, scattered, or anxious, and a sense of feeling lost in the world. In times of financial worry, the 1st chakra can be triggered bringing about imbalance as well.

2nd Chakra (Swadhistana)- The 2nd chakra is referred to as the *sacral chakra* and is located near the sacrum. It relates to our emotions, sexuality, creativity, and passion. This chakra corresponds with the reproductive organs, the elimination organs, such as lower intestines, kidneys, and urinary tract. Traumas that occur in childhood often get stuck in the second chakra. It tends to be the storehouse for repressed or traumatic emotions.

3rd Chakra (Manipura)- The 3rd chakra, or *solar plexus chakra*, is related to our sense of self-confidence and power. If we feel insecure, then our third chakra is out of balance. The flip side of the coin is feeling arrogant and controlling. This is also a byproduct of insecurity and a third chakra imbalance. Because the 3rd chakra relates to how we use our energy, it relates to the digestive organs. Third chakra imbalances most commonly show up in our 20s when we our independent and on our own for the first time.

4th Chakra (Anahata)- The 4th chakra, also referred to as the *heart chakra*, is located at the physical heart. It correlates to how we relate to others and is associated with love for others, self-love, and compassion. In cases of a "broken heart," the 4th chakra will feel the brunt of this emotion. Other common emotions held in the fourth chakra are resentment, bitterness, coldness, and fear. The 4th chakra is also linked to following our heart's desires or passions in life. When the 4th chakra is open, we have more clarity in life. Our heart is our true compass, not the mind.

5th Chakra (Vishuddha)- The 5th chakra, also known as the *throat chakra*, is located at the throat. Not surprisingly, it relates to our communication and expression. Have you ever felt like someone put a sock down your throat, felt tongue-tied, or like you were misunderstood? These imbalances relate to the 5th chakra. Our forms of expression can be through speaking, writing, cooking, dancing, or any other form. While the passion originates in the 2nd chakra, it is expressed through the 5th chakra.

You can imagine then how important the 3rd and 4th chakras are in the full spectrum of how we manifest our ideas into the world. In fact, the throat chakra is the bridge between the spiritual and physical world. When we don't have an adequate outlet for expressing ourselves, this could result in shoulder tension, throat issues, and thyroid imbalance. Over time, it can put emotional and physical pressure on the heart as well.

6th Chakra (Ajna)- The 6th chakra, is commonly referred to as the *third eye* because it is located between the two eyebrows. This chakra is related to visualizing, imagining, and dreaming. It is associated with the pineal gland, which is linked to our intuition. When the 6th eye chakra is open, we are more in tune psychically and with our dreams. This chakra also helps to balance the right and left brains. Headaches and migraines are common signs of an imbalance of the 6th chakra.

7th Chakra (Sahasrara)- The 7th chakra, also referred to as the *crown chakra*, is located at the top of the head. It is often symbolized by a thousand-petal lotus and located on the crown of the head. This chakra is our connection to higher consciousness, overall wisdom, oneness, and to Source, or God. It is linked to the pituitary gland and relates to the brain functions.

Inanimate Objects Have Feelings Too

It is commonly accepted in physics that all beings and objects are composed of vibrating atoms and therefore emit an energy field. How a non-living entity responds or conducts the energy depends upon its properties, such as its shape, color, and composition. For example, a red, round ball will respond to the energy differently than a yellow, square cube. A rolling hill will respond differently than a jagged cliff. Whereas, the energy of a living entity will be more determined by its state of consciousness in coordination with thoughts and emotions.

Just as humans can affect each other's energy fields, the same is true with inanimate objects. The most obvious example is electronic components, such as televisions, phones, and computers that transmit electromagnetic waves. It has been proven that excessive and concentrated exposure to electromagnetic waves can cause fatigue, sickness, and depression. Because we emit electromagnetic waves, there is a resonance and our energy can affect electronics as well.

This may seem far-fetched at first, but many of us already intuitively acknowledge this. Have you ever talked to an inanimate object in the form of a 'pep talk' to help it work properly? For example, your car is having a hard time starting and so you begin saying, "Come on, come on, come on!" Maybe you even give it a morale booster, such as, "You can do it!"

My iTunes is another great example. I have a large variety of musical genres stored on my phone, ranging from New Age to Jazz to Alternative Rock, and it automatically shuffles to an energy that matches my energy. It's also not coincidental that people who hate technology always have technology problems, whereas those who love technology never have technical glitches.

It's not just electronics that are sensitive to energy. It just so happens that they are more equipped to communicate back to us. Any object will take on our energy. The more time we spend with certain objects, such as our car or a personal object such as a ring, the more affected it will be by our energy. Psychics or intuitives can usually read a person's energy by holding a personal item. This is known as *psychometry*. An energy field around an object will hold the energy projected at it, similar to a memory. Each time that same thought or emotion is projected on the object, the stronger it will be to where one will automatically pick up that emotion just by being near the object. Psychometry applies to everything in a house, including décor items, the walls, and furniture.

Furniture

Just as your jewelry and photos hold energy, so does your furniture. It is therefore important to not only space clear your home, but your furniture too, particularly antiques. I remember as a kid having an extreme aversion to going into antique stores. I would feel claustrophobic in the store and usually had to go outside. When selecting furnishings for a children's room, keep in mind that they are more sensitive than adults. Even today when I go to a consignment or antique store, I have to pull in my energy field and browse quickly.

If you bring an antique piece of furniture into your home, keep in mind that you are also bringing in energy from its past into your home. Some people love having these slices of history in their home and may even characterize themselves as a historian of sorts. If this is you then just be conscious of the energy in your home and how you feel. When a new piece is purchased and displayed, notice if the room feels different. Be aware of any unexplainable mood shifts within yourself. It is also recommended to smudge furniture just as you would space clear your home. This will help to clear the old energy and minimize its effect on you and your home's energy.

Whether new or old, furniture can be one of the most disguised forms of clutter. We usually think of clutter as being small items stuffed in the back of a closet, not an ornate armoire that costs thousands of dollars. While we need furniture to sit on, sleep on, and eat on, it can clog up a floor plan quicker than anything else. You may have an ideal feng shui floor plan, but too much furniture can reverse the benefits. Having too much furniture will cut off the flow and breath of the space.

Furniture seems to bring up a lot of emotion for people. One of my client's homes was filled with antique chairs passed down from family members. There was enough seating in her home to fit a small army. Although she admits that she has too many chairs for the space, she can't imagine getting rid of any of them because they are all family pieces. No other family members wanted the chairs so she agreed to take them.

Be conscious of whether you are the family's dumping ground for unwanted pieces of furniture. Most of us feel guilty about getting rid of family pieces that we don't want, so instead we find a family member who will take them. Don't be that person, unless you really want and can use the piece of furniture.

The thought of getting rid of furniture is anathema for certain generations. Furniture was passed down as heirloom pieces, particularly bedroom suites. It was at a time when furniture was handmade, expensive, and those with nice pieces felt grateful. In my generation and younger, we buy and sell furniture on Craigslist like we would any other commodity. And now that furniture is mass-produced by companies such as IKEA, we don't think twice about getting rid of a dresser because it no longer goes with our current style.

Just like a floor plan, the arrangement of furniture should allow the energy to meander. Notice if there are pieces of furniture that you routinely run into. I once worked in an office with a desk that was too big for the space. The entire time I worked there I had a permanent bruise on my right hip from bumping into the corner of the desk. Notice if there are areas in your home that feel tight or cramped. Notice your breathing and how it changes when walking in areas with lots of furniture and areas with fewer pieces. In placing furniture, here are a few tips to keep in mind:

- Avoid placing furniture in hallways.
- Allow at least three-foot walkthrough space in transition areas.

- Avoid placing furniture at a diagonal, except in certain cases where it is necessary.
- Minimize furniture with sharp corners. Opt for rounded corners instead.
- Reconsider using furniture from childhood, particularly bedroom furniture.
- Find the focal point of the room, i.e. fireplace, and arrange furniture accordingly.

If you feel like the walls are closing in on you or that your breathing is labored, then you might have too much furniture. Many clients report that they feel like the walls are coming in on them in all areas of their life. This is usually indicative of too much furniture and other clutter. On the flip side, I occasionally come across homes with too few furniture pieces and other décor items. In such cases, the space will feel cold, impersonal and ungrounded.

Clutter and the Art of Detaching

As a result of mass production in the 20th century, our economic system changed to a consumer model and our appetite for buying stuff is insatiable. The economic crash in 2008 gave us all pause before making a purchase. As a society, we have become more conscious of what we bring into our homes and what we need to take out of our homes. People now realize that they don't feel good with too much stuff. As a result, the urge to purge or declutter our homes has become as common as decorating.

One of my favorite quotes is by 19th century interior designer, William Morris, that says: "Have nothing in your house that you do not know to be useful, or believe to be beautiful." But this is often easier said than done. It's not always as easy as making some runs to Goodwill. There is often an emotional component that outweighs the simple logistics of clearing clutter. This emotional attachment is explored in great detail in my book, *Clutter Intervention: How Your Stuff is Keeping You Stuck*.

Buying and accumulating stuff is just another way to distract ourselves from our present lives. Like cigarettes or alcohol, our stuff is a quick fix to feeling good. When the high wears off, we are left with an icky feeling. Is this an overreaction to buying a new toaster? Maybe. But consumption can be an addiction that is hard to recognize because it is so socially affirmed by our friends, family, media, and government. Extreme cases of overconsumption may be diagnosed as hoarding.[9]

Knowing why we are attached to certain items will often break the emotional attachment with our stuff. For some of us, having a lot of stuff is simply a distraction from our everyday life. A cluttered space results in a cluttered mind, which is exactly what some of us want, *at least subconsciously*. In the same way alcohol makes things fuzzy, having a lot of things in your space will do the same. And on some level, that may be the desired outcome.

It's not always the quantity of stuff you have, so much as the emotions you are hanging onto. I had one client whose home was immaculate and she prided herself as being a minimalist and clutter-free. She was interested in using feng shui to help attract a love relationship. Her house felt very comfortable and she had an inherent knack for feng shui. That is, until I went into her bedroom. Not only did she have images and shapes with the number *1* in them (a feng shui *no-no* in the bedroom as it signifies being single), but she had a stack of yearbooks sitting on her dresser and a stuffed animal from childhood on her bed.

Her closets were completely clear of clutter, but the few items that she was hanging onto spoke volumes based on where the clutter was located and displayed. Hanging onto her childhood and high school years was keeping her anchored in the past and preventing her from moving

---

[9] If you believe you or a family member suffers from hoarding, you should contact a mental health professional. Hoarding is closely associated with Obsessive Control Disorder and other mental disorders, although it has now been classified in the DSM-V as its own separate diagnosis. Similar to the difference between social drinking and alcoholism, so is the case with shopping and hoarding. When it comes to the point where it interferes with work and relationships, then it may have crossed the line and medical help may be appropriate.

forward. While it is fine to keep memorabilia such as this, be conscious of whether it is keeping you in the past, or not.

We all have our particular Achilles heel when it comes to hanging onto items. For some it may be books or magazines. For others, it may be Tupperware containers and kitchen gadgets. And for others, it is clothing and jewelry. For these items that trigger us, we will come up with the most imaginative and creative reasons to hang onto them.

In a clutter clearing workshop I held, I asked participants to bring an item that was hard for them to let go of. A woman in her late 60's with short hair brought in a box of hundreds of hairbands. She was keeping them "just in case." After some discussion, she realized that she was keeping them because they reminded her of her youth when she had long, flowing hair. Upon this realization, she was able to release the box of hairbands, but kept one of them for purposes of memorabilia.

If you are hanging on to an item or items that you know you don't love or use, but still can't part with, then it's time to acknowledge an emotional attachment to the item(s).

With regard to a particular item, ask yourself these questions:

What am I feeling right now?
What memories does this item bring up?
Who gave it to me?
Why did I originally buy it?
Who does it remind me of?
Do I feel guilty getting rid of this item? If so, why?
Why? Why? And Why?

Be your own detective. If it brings up too much emotion, then consult a counselor or put the item away for the next round of decluttering. It may be too soon to part with it. Once you realize why you are hanging on to an item, it's usually pretty easy to let it go. It's almost magically easy. You may be surprised. What you thought was just an old hairbrush may actually be a reservoir of past emotions that you and your sister shared when she helped you get ready for prom. Or maybe the green gingham shirt with the price tag on it conjures up guilt for buying things that are on sale and never wearing them. Until acknowledged, the shirt will hang in your closet serving only to attract the pattern for more guilt.

It's never just about the item itself. It's the emotion the item holds. And so it's not about detaching from the item, per se. It's about acknowledging and feeling the emotion that you have stored away in this item. The item is only there as a representation for the emotions and once processed it will be ready to move on. Make peace with it in the form of crying, forgiving, remembering, or resolving. Say *Thank You and Goodbye* to honor the item and yourself. If you have the awareness but still don't want to get rid of the item, then it may simply be too early. See how you feel the next round of decluttering.

To start the process of decluttering, work in baby steps. In doing so, you will build up the confidence that will keep you going through the long haul. Once you realize that life will go on with fewer items, you will not only want to clear out more stuff, but will start to feel a freedom in your mind and your body. And when you feel this sense of freedom you know you have mastered the art of detaching from your stuff.

Objects of Our Expression

Each and every object in our home is a personalization of us. Even items that seem purely functional, such as your kitchen potato peeler, are expressions of you on some level. Is it a new, ergonomic gadget or a traditional, basic peeler that reminds you of the one your mother used? Decorative items sitting on your mantel are expressions of your personality. Or maybe they hold a deeper meaning and emotions, such as family photos or ashes of a loved one.

In the book, *House as a Mirror of Self*, the author conducted numerous interviews and studies of real households in order to find correlations between the owners and their space. What she found was that the movable objects in the home were the most powerful representations of people. It is no wonder that splitting up belongings at the end of a relationship is often the most painful part. These objects hold the energy of the couple. When the items are divvied up, an energy cord is being cut between the couple mirroring the relationship.

The importance of our objects can also be seen when moving. Nothing brings to the surface the importance, or lack thereof, of our stuff more so than when we move. When it comes time to pack, we come face-to-face with all of our stuff. This, in and of itself, prevents some people from moving at all. They are overwhelmed with the memories contained in their belongings and choose not to face it.

When we move, we consciously pick and choose what items we want to take with us into our next chapter. We pack those items that are most important to us. These items also help ground us into our next home. Think back to the last time you moved into a new space. The home was unfamiliar, perhaps even a little scary. You then unpack your first box. You see the familiarity of your dishes or your favorite books.

With each box unpacked, you start to feel at home. As we get more and more settled over the first few weeks of living in our new home, our energy starts to settle into the home. New patterns emerge - ranging from where we place art and photos to where we sit to have morning coffee. Conversely, we start to take on the unique energy of the space, including the floor plan, shape, numerology, and any predecessor energy. Before long, we have entered into a new relationship with the space, which becomes a mirror of ourselves.

PART II

YOUR HOME SPEAKS YOUR MIND

*House, patch of meadow, oh evening
light Suddenly you acquire an almost
human face You are very near us, embracing
and embraced.*

—Ranier Maria Rilke

Soon after moving in and settling into your new home, your energy and that of your home begin to merge. As you unpack, arrange the furniture, decorate, and hang your favorite picture, your energy begins to settle into the home. Simultaneously, your energy starts to meld into the energy of the home. As you become acquainted with the floor plan and which light switch turns on which light, the newness of the space starts to wear off. Our home starts to feel intuitive to our energy similar to a bird's nest fitting the shape of its bird. We feel at home.

We start new habits, patterns, and routines in our new home as we adjust to the new space. And your personal energy starts to take root and housed in your home. Over time, the energy of your home will begin to shape areas of your life. And your energy will manifest around your home through your subconscious mind in the form of symbols and messages. This intimate connection can be seen throughout your home as if it were a mirror.

When things out of the ordinary break, become damaged, or need repairing, these are symbolic messages from our subconscious. Just as a mind-body book may guide you to understand why you are experiencing a certain illness, pain, or disease, Part II will show you why certain occurrences are happening within your home. Each aspect of the home represents a certain aspect of ourselves. For example, when something breaks down, it is indicative of the correlating aspect within ourselves breaking down or in need of attention. Similarly, when you make repairs or improvements, the correlating change takes place within yourself.

Part II decodes the most common messages from your home starting at the foundation. Each aspect of the house symbolizes some aspect of one's self, including rooms, mechanicals, components, and outdoor areas of the home from the ground up and extending to the exterior of the home. With the variety of spaces available - from lofts to boats to shared spaces - not every space will contain all the components, parts, and rooms included within this section. Notwithstanding, most of these symbolic references will show up somewhere in your life. For example, if you don't have a basement, your equivalent may instead be located in the garage, a closet, or even an off-site storage facility.

Just as our body sends us messages from our subconscious mind, so does our home. What is your home saying about your physical health, emotional and mental well-being, or spiritual growth? For example, if you have a clogged toilet, you can pull the book off the shelf, go to the Plumbing section, and see what correlating aspect is going on within yourself. (Then, call the plumber.) You will be able to access all of this information and bring to light your own subconscious mind. Become the architect of your soul by building, renovating, or simply decorating your life.

CHAPTER 7

THE LANGUAGE OF THE HOME

I built the house in sections, always following the concrete needs of the moment.... Only afterward did I see how all the parts fitted together and that a meaningful form had resulted: a symbol of psychic wholeness.

—Carl Jung

Every facet of our home is a symbolic representation of our physical, mental, emotional, and/or spiritual Self. In understanding and recognizing these correlations, our home can provide us with a wealth of insight about ourselves as well as opportunities to make changes in our life. These correlations come to us from the home in the form of symbols. It is not coincidental that the language of our subconscious mind is through symbols and images.

Symbols are metaphorical images that are representative of a bigger meaning. They are in effect a universal language. Similar to a picture being worth a thousand words, symbols can say a lot more and give us a deeper meaning than words. Because symbols appear to us in the form of images or pictures, on some level we recognize them and have an intuitive understanding of their meaning through our collective consciousness.

Symbols are most often associated with our dreams. Dream symbols are usually considered archetypes because they are common among all of us through our collective conscious. Our subconscious intuitively taps into the collective conscious of humans in present time and those who came before us. Most symbols therefore have the same meaning to us as everyone else, particularly within the same cultures. Because a symbol has endured the same meaning for thousands of years, it also carries a certain energy, or vibration. This is also the reason we are able to interpret our dreams from common dream dictionaries.

Symbols can also appear as personal symbols, instead of archetypes. For instance, if someone was traumatically stung by a stingray as a child, then being chased by a stingray in their dream would most likely take on a different meaning than it does for most others. Also, certain cultures, religions, and geographical variations can account for different meanings. For example, an image of Santa Claus will not have the meaning of a benevolent giver for everyone, given their culture, religion, or even a personal experience one may have had as a child with Santa Claus. So, while we are all connected to the Universal Mind or collective consciousness, we each have our own individualized and historical variations within making our experience unique.

Because our subconscious mind thinks in terms of images, we dream in pictures, which are in effect symbols. With these pictures, our dreams are reflecting back to us our subconscious mind. This could be repressed thoughts or simply an unloading of garbage that our subconscious mind picked over the day. Afterall, our subconscious mind is working at an infinitesimal rate compared to that of our conscious mind.

Usually our dreams send us messages to our conscious mind of which we may not be consciously aware. For example, suppose someone hates going to work because they feel like they don't fit in. The subconscious mind knows the underlying truth of the situation is the pattern of playing a victim, or feeling victimized. Because the subconscious communicates through pictures, the dream may look something like being chased by sharks in the ocean. Our dreams are rarely as direct as your boss walking up to you saying, "as usual, you're being a victim!" Instead our subconscious communicates in terms of symbols, images, and energy. The energy and imagery of the sharks is more powerful in showing us the emotions we are experiencing at work in this example. It is also helpful to our understanding of ourself if we are taken out of our daily life. Only then can we be more objective to what we are experiencing in our waking life.

When someone communicates information to us using stories or metaphors, the meaning comes through because we can identify with it using our frame of reference or experiences. In doing so, we recognize the lesson or message on a more conscious level and are more likely to act on it. This is the same reason our dreams play out as a metaphorical story. It is a way to "reach" us indirectly and non-aggressively. Sometimes, it is so indirect that it seems like someone else's story. For example, the shark is chasing your sister and you therefore think the dream is about her. But, this is just another way your subconscious mind is trying to show you your story.

Dreams can offer us powerful opportunities for healing. In addition to helping us see a situation more objectively, dreams can allow us to practice for real life. We often use dreams to play out different scenarios before we do so in real life. Dreams can also help us overcome patterns. In the example above, the dream may have continued with the dreamer seeing the shark turn into a frog, a symbol of transformation. Or, perhaps the dream plays out to where the he or she stands up to the shark.

Dreams can also be a red flag of something we were totally unaware. This is the case with prophetic dreams. Because our subconscious mind is constantly recording everything, it picks up and knows things before our conscious mind does. Our subconscious mind makes up 83% of our brain and controls 96-98% of perception and behavior.[10] It processes 400 billion bits of information per second compared to the conscious

---

[10] John Assaraf & Murray Smith, *The Answer*, p. 48 (Atria Paperback 2009).

brain's mere 2000 bits of information per second.[11] When we are finally still with all of our systems in temporary hibernation mode during sleep, the subconscious is finally able to communicate to us. In fact, it is not uncommon for people to have dreams alerting them of a particular illness of which they were otherwise unaware.

Dream symbols pertaining to the home are also common. Since the beginning of dream interpretation, the house and its components have represented aspects of the Self. The house is an archetypal symbol for the Self, or Soul. I often have what I call 'home dreams' that convey information about my health and well-being through symbols of the home. For example, in one dream, the exact right half of the home was being completely renovated, while I was only living in the left side of the home. It was as if a line had been drawn down the middle. This was a representation of the left and right sides of my brain. At that time, I was transitioning from practicing law to the healing arts where I was starting to use my right brain on a whole new level. My right brain was undergoing a renovation.

A few years ago, I was able to use my dreams to help diagnose abdominal pains that I was having. I had to wait about a week before I could get a doctor's appointment and ultrasound. In the meantime, I had a series of three dreams that showed me the problem through symbolic interior images of homes. In addition, the people and the storylines of the dream helped me understand the mind-body relationship of the underlying problem.

Symbols not only appear in dreams, but also in our waking life. The only difference is that we usually don't notice these signs and symbols in our waking lives as we do in our subconscious dream state. For example, perhaps you take the afternoon off and go to the park. As you start walking you come upon a pond and notice a school of fish swimming. Even though you have walked by the same pond numerous times, this is the first time you have noticed fish swimming. Seeing the fish swimming

---

[11] Id.

in a pond in waking life may not trigger anything out of the ordinary because it has a normal context. Our logical, rational mind just brushes it away.

However, if you see the same thing in a dream, then you may wonder why you are seeing a school of fish. If this still isn't enough to get your attention, perhaps the next time the fish will be chasing you. In all instances, however, seeing the school of fish symbolizes that certain things have been surfacing or are being revealed from your subconscious mind to your conscious mind. Unless we are consciously looking for them, the signs and symbols in our waking life usually don't get our attention like those in our dream state. Either way, however, the meanings are the same.

In the book *Sixth Sense*, author Stuart Wilde explains that external symbols (or symbols in our waking life) will be grouped together. For example, you'll see a man fall off his bike and later that day, you will see a tile fall off a roof and hit a truck. The point of these grouped symbols is to see a larger theme. In this example, the theme or message would be balance. What do you need to balance in your life? Wilde also makes the point that waking symbols will often show up in your dreams as well. They are messages from your subconscious mind trying to get the attention of your conscious mind.

Our subconscious mind picks up on things in our environment of which we are not consciously aware. For example, a friend of mine sat at a wood desk that was teetering on a broken leg for about a year. Each and every day that she worked at the desk, her subconscious mind registered the broken leg. Even though she wasn't thinking about it consciously, it was impacting her subconscious mind. Then, one day she had a random accident at home, breaking her own leg. Not coincidentally, while she was out of work recovering, a co-worker finally got around to wood-gluing the desk's broken leg. She came back to works months later to a sturdy work desk.

In any space in which we spend a lot of time, our subconscious mind will constantly pick up on things in our environment whether we are consciously aware of them or not. This is why our environment whether it is our home, office, or car, impacts us so greatly. While a messy car, desk, or kitchen may consciously drive you crazy, just think how your subconscious mind is responding. By living more consciously in the present moment, we can begin to tune into these symbols throughout our day and in our home.

As our body is a manifestation of our mind, the home is the next closest extension of our mind and body. As you delve into the following chapters, you will start to make the connections with yourself and the different areas of your home. Your experience may coincide with the symbols that are a part of our collective consciousness, or you may have your own personal experience that is completely different based on your past associations. You will begin to decode the language of your home as it actually speaks your mind. And as you make changes to your home, you will also see correlating changes take place within yourself.

CHAPTER 8

FLOORS - LEVELS OF CONSCIOUSNESS

I always thought of myself as a house. I was always what I lived in. It didn't need to be big. It didn't even need to be beautiful. It just needed to be mine. I became what I was meant to be. I built myself a life. I built myself a house.

—George in Life as a House

- Foundation
- Basement
- Main Level
- 2nd Floor
- Attic

In the 2001 movie, *Life as a House*, the main character, played by Kevin Kline, embarks on building a house while battling cancer and mending a troubled relationship with his son. Their relationship was slowly built just as the house was – one floor at a time starting with the foundation. Whether building a relationship or a house, it is essential to build a strong foundation before moving to the higher floors.

On the energetic level, each floor of the house represents a different level of consciousness. This metaphor was depicted in the movie, *Inception*. While Leonardo DiCaprio was in a constant struggle to determine which reality was 'real,' he would travel up and down the floors of his consciousness via an elevator. The lower down he traveled in the elevator, the deeper he went into his subconscious mind.

In Iyanla Vanzant's self-help book, *In the Meantime*, she organizes the chapters according to the floors of a house working from the bottom up in order to "clean house" before entering a new relationship. Likewise, she uses each floor metaphorically to represent each level of consciousness. In all of these examples, the lower floors represent our lower subconscious mind while the higher floors represent our higher levels of consciousness. Just like building a house, let's start with the foundation and work our way up.

Foundation

To build anything with integrity, especially a house, it must have a strong foundation. The foundation of the home literally represents our foundation or grounding. This relates to the First Chakra. The foundation is in direct contact with the Earth and the Earth's energy. The more solid and secure the foundation of your home, the more grounding you will experience while living there. There are many clichés that we already use in our everyday language that point to this. For example, "having a strong foundation" is often used with regard to starting a new relationship, project, business, or anything with a new beginning. It is common knowledge that we have to "build a strong foundation" to make anything worthwhile last or succeed.

There are several factors in determining how well a home's foundation is built.

The actual ground or land on which the foundation is built is an important factor affecting the strength of the whole house. Whether you are building or buying a home, take time to inspect the ground to determine if it will make a proper foundation. In states in earthquake zones, this is required. But, otherwise, call in a professional if you are unsure.

What is the topography of the land? Will it be conducive to proper water drainage? Is the mineral composition proper for a foundation? I once had a contract on a home that seemed like the perfect home. I was swept off my feet by the beautiful screened-in porch off the back. Upon receiving the termite report, however, I realized that this home was not for me. It had had severe damage in the past to the point of having a structural engineer reconfigure the foundation. Not only that, but the home showed current termite activity despite having been treated annually.

Ironically, I ended up purchasing the home next door that never had any issues with termites. There was something about the conditions of the ground and the home itself that attracted the termites. Luckily, I was able to discover the truth before purchasing it. Unfortunately however, sometimes you don't know what lies below. One client, upon excavation, ran into the remnants of a previous structure on the lot – an old nursing home.

'Settling' Into Your Home

It is common for houses to naturally "settle" over time as the foundation sinks farther into the ground. The settling should be done naturally and gently, otherwise the house may undergo structural damage. If a home has foundation problems, that energy will be felt throughout the house and affect its occupants on an energetic level until or unless the foundation is corrected. Its occupants may struggle with laying a proper foundation in relationships or projects. Another challenge may be a lack of proper energy flow in the lower chakras, which will lead to over-activity in the mind in the form of worry and anxiety, as well as physical problems in the legs and feet.

People, couples, or businesses without a strong foundation may attract a house or space with foundation problems due to a vibrational match of their own lack of grounding. This will continue until the owner is forced to either remedy the problem or move. By this point, it is likely that the occupants are going through their own breakdown of sorts, physically, mentally or emotionally. Because the foundation affects the entire house, it will correlate with a major shakeup in the lives of its occupants.

If the owner has the financial resources to do so, it can be beneficial for the homeowner to go through this time with the home instead of escaping it by moving. In doing so, there is an opportunity to make a major transformation in not only the home, but their life as well. For example, if the owners are having marital problems, then fixing the foundation may help the couple rebuild their relationship as well, perhaps in the form of couple's therapy.

A house with previous foundation problems that have since been fixed will hold the energy of transformation. Because the house has undergone a transformation itself, it will have that effect on its inhabitants. This was the case with my previous home. Being an unusually heavy cast concrete home, it settled in a less than gentle manner resulting in foundation problems. A telltale sign of a home settling is visible hairline cracks on the interior drywall or exterior masonry of the home. You might also see a gap between the home and front porch or a gap between the bathtub and tile splash around it.

The front section of this particular house had settled quicker than the rest of the home. Previous owners had remedied the problem by putting extra supports under this portion. Nevertheless, the front door frame remained slightly off causing a structural and energetic mismatch around this area. Not coincidentally, one of the areas of personal growth for me while living in this house was the importance of building a strong foundation in personal relationships, which carried over into other areas of my life as well.

Just like ourselves, no home is perfect and many homes have or have had foundation problems. The important point is to be conscious of your home's foundation. Because the foundation of your home affects the entire home, it is structurally the most important part of the house. An unstable foundation in your home can lead to uncertainty or instability in other areas of your life.

If you knowingly buy a house, perhaps a fixer-upper, with a foundation issue, then know that this is your opportunity for transformation. Avoid purchasing a home with foundation problems without the intent of remedying the problem. Ideally, select a house with a strong foundation. This will carry through into your life. It is always easier to walk on smooth pavement than gravel. This is the same with the foundation of a home. A home with a strong foundation will help you build strong foundations in every area of your life.

Mind Body Home Connection: Foundation
- What is the topography of the land? Is it sloped or flat?
- What is the ground composition, i.e. sand, dirt, clay, etc.
- How deeply rooted into the Earth is the foundation of your home?
- How well do you handle the 'storms' in your life?
- Do you feel like you have a strong foundation or support system in your life?
- Do you feel supported?
- Do you feel grounded or do you feel like you're walking on unsteady or shaky ground?
- How well do you handle stressful situations or events?
- Are you anxious for no reason or over small things?
- Have you undergone or undergoing a major 'breakdown' or foundational shake-up in your life?
- Has your home been remedied of foundation problems prior to you living there?

Basement

A basement is generally defined as that part of the house that is below or at least partially below ground. Basements are, generally speaking, either built out to be living spaces, concreted in, or left as the natural earth. Unless a house is built on a slab or has a crawl space, then the basement directly connects to the ground. The basement is usually accessible from the main living floor, but not a frequently trafficked area of the home. It is the metaphorical action of walking down the stairs to access the basement that makes it energetically unique to all other floors in the house.

The subterranean basement represents our subconscious mind and suppressed emotions. On the mental level, our subconscious mind is a vast space where we store lots of information, memories, and emotions. Although we can access our subconscious mind, we often are not aware of what's down there. Perhaps this is similar to your basement.

While our subconscious mind processes an impressive amount of data 24/7, it also happens to be where we store our perceived faults and shortcomings. These are often referred to as our subconscious minefields, blocks, or saboteurs. These subconscious blocks are usually based in negative beliefs about ourselves that stem from childhood. Common beliefs often include not being good enough, pretty enough, smart enough, athletic enough, or any other 'not good enough' negative message picked up or perceived over time.

The more aware or conscious we are about our subconscious beliefs, the more aligned we will ultimately be with the life we want. For example, if you consciously want a certain job, but subconsciously don't think you are good enough for the position, then you most likely won't get the job. Right in the middle of the interview, your subconscious minefield will get triggered and you will say something that sabotages the interview. Or maybe you simply come into the interview without adequate self-confidence, which gets picked up by the interviewer.

Our subconscious mind can also save us at times as it also holds our positive truths as well. Perhaps you think you want the job, but subconsciously you really don't or maybe it's simply not in your best interest. Your subconscious mind will try to get your attention in some way. What appears to be self-sabotage, for example, showing up late or not sending in the application at all, may really be your subconscious sending you messages.

What's Really Down There?

You may be wondering what this has to do with your basement? Whatever you are storing in your basement has a direct correlation to what you are storing in your subconscious mind. We usually store things in our basement that we don't need to access frequently, or perhaps ever at all. We often store things in the basement that we don't want to deal with at the time. And then there are those functional items that we only need occasionally. But for the most part, we put stuff in the basement that we either don't have space for in other parts of the home or want out of our visual sight. Nonetheless, all of the stuff in your basement is stored in your subconscious mind and energetically in your body on some energetic level.

If you want to know what you are storing in your subconscious, take a look in your basement. First notice the overall quantity and arrangement of stuff in your basement. Is it neat and organized? Or, is it so messy you don't even know what's down there anymore? Notice the type of items you store in your basement. Do they tend to be memorabilia, pragmatic tools, or remnants of old hobbies? Do you store old photo albums or yearbooks? Or are you storing things that you no longer even need? Is the basement where you store items that are difficult to let go?

The basement is a common place to store items that relate to an old identity. An identity that no longer relates to our current life can be energetically held and prevent us from moving forward in life. The energy around an identity can be stuck by simply holding on to items relating to that time of life. For example, an old varsity jacket may remind you of an era in which you were youthful, popular, or an athlete. A photo album full of pictures could represent unresolved feelings and identity around being a wife, grandchild, basketball star, or a girlfriend. Or your grandmother's old piano may remind you of when you were a child.

Whether you need to get rid of items in your basement depends on you. Do you dread going down into the basement? If so, acknowledge why. Acknowledge what feelings are associated with items that you are holding onto. Be as objective as possible as to whether that item is holding you back, anchoring you to the past, or if it simply doesn't make you feel good. Be conscious of why you are keeping an item. If it is still serving you in some way, then continue storing in the basement. Otherwise, it may be time to let it go.

What if your home has no basement, or just a crawl space? You, of course, still have a subconscious mind, but you may not be storing as much stuff as those with a basement. In other words, everything is forced to come to the surface to deal with in present time. My client, Terry, was renting a guesthouse with no basement or storage space. The entire year she lived there, she was purging her past by clearing out items she once stored away out of sight. She was forced to face her past as there was no place to hide it any longer. By the end of the year, she completely purged all that she needed to release.

Basements and Boundaries

The basement can often become a place of refuge for other people's stuff, such as items left by previous owners, inherited items, your children's stored items, or god forbid your neighbor's junk or ex's leftovers. Unless a clear boundary is drawn as to how long and why someone is storing items in your home, then it can represent a lack of boundaries altogether. By storing other people's stuff, you are allowing other people to take your energy.

I was guilty of this myself when I naively purchased my second home. It had a dirt basement that came with multiple previous owners' leftover junk. As much as I loved the house, I dreaded going into the basement and always felt unsettled with what lied beneath me. During the five years I lived there, I never really knew what was down there besides the few square feet I had taken up just at the bottom of the stairs with paint supplies. Having other people's stuff in my basement was representative of how I allowed other people to impose or influence me without setting adequate boundaries. I was allowing people to take up my space (my energy) with their stuff (their energy).

This became clear to me when I was getting ready to sell the house and had to clean out the basement. For two days, I worked underground in this basement to clear out decades of emotions that had been stored in this home. Although most of the stuff wasn't even mine, it was as if I had cleared my own subconscious mind of anything old, decrepit, musty, and unused. It was truly a dirty job and I emerged out of the dark basement into the light as a different person. The house felt amazing and I had wished I had done it much sooner. From then on, I was much better about setting boundaries, taking up my own energy, and making sure my future homes were clear of the previous owner's stuff before taking possession.

The lines get a little more blurred when it involves family members. We want to be generous and considerate of our family members' things. But it can come to the point to where enough is enough. I see this often with clients who are storing things for their children in case they want items later in life. At the same time, they are storing inherited items from their parents for themselves or siblings. Before they know it, they feel like the walls are coming in on them. So while you want to be considerate of family members - dead or alive - you must also be aware of what is in your best interest as well. Don't become your family's dumping ground for guilt-ridden items.

Basements and Flooding

On the weekend of May 1, 2010, Nashville experienced massive flooding that, according to records, happens once every thousand years. I lived in Nashville at the time and saw first-hand the devastation. Thousands of people were forced to come face-to-face with the stuff in their basement. The yards and streets looked as if houses had purged all of their belongings as the contents were either lying out to dry or stacked up for trash. It was appalling to see how much stuff we as a society accumulate and how needless it really is at the end of the day.

As a result of the flood, there was a massive clearing of old subconscious beliefs across the mid-South. Nature forced thousands of people to declutter their basements and to face their shadow sides lurking within their subconscious. So was the case with the city of Nashville itself as so many of its landmark buildings were cleared out as well from the flood.

Even those who didn't sustain damage were inspired to clean out their basements as well. In the months and years following the flood, I spoke with many people who expressed how much better they felt after forced to clean out their basement. For some, they said it was the best thing that could have happened as they feel so much better as a result.

Out of Sight, Out of Mind?

Another possibility is that you have found other creative locations to store items that you would otherwise store in your basement. If your home doesn't have a basement, then consider where else you might be storing items that could hold the key to unlocking your subconscious. Is it in the closets, garage, or storage shed? If so, read on to see what section of the house those areas signify. Just because you can't see it, doesn't mean it's not affecting you. In fact, the more you try to hide it, the more in denial or out of touch you are with your emotions. Storing items in off-site storage, a friend's home, or your ex-husband's home is detaching from an aspect of yourself and giving your power away.

There are of course transition times in our life when storing off-site is necessary. But it should be considered a temporary solution, not permanent. Of course, storing items is not always a bad thing either. It certainly can serve a useful and functional purpose. However, it should be done *consciously*. Be mindful of each item you are storing and why. The more in alignment your subconscious mind is with your conscious mind, the more in alignment you will be with your true self. If you feel stagnant in any area of your life, then letting go of some items in your basement is a great start. Holding items from the past keeps us in the past. When you let go of items from the past, it creates space for new energy and new memories to come into your life.

Mind Body Home Connection: **Basement**

- Do you have a full basement, partial basement, crawl space, or slab?
- What are you storing in your basement?
- Are you storing memorabilia from your past? Is it from happy times or not-so-happy times?
- Are you overwhelmed with the amount of stuff in your basement?
- Are you storing other peoples' stuff? If so, why?
- Are you storing "just-in-case" items? If so, is it a realistic contingency?
- Are there items that you would like to get rid of?

Main Level

Every home has a main or primary level on which most of the activity of everyday living takes place. The main floor is usually the floor into which the front door opens. One exception is split-level homes. In a split-level home, occupants are often conflicted in life and feel torn in two different directions. Nevertheless, the floor that gets used the most – usually containing the kitchen and living room – would be considered the main living floor. For a single-story home, all living spaces are located on the main level. Because the front door enters into the main level, it is the floor with the most active energy. The main floor is closely aligned with the 3rd Chakra, our power center.

The main living floor represents our present state of consciousness. It is a reflection of our day-to-day life and personality. In *The Book of Secrets*, Deepak Chopra says, "It's possible to scan someone's personal space and fairly accurately discern if that person is satisfied or dissatisfied with life, has a strong or weak sense of personal identity, is a conformist or nonconformist, values order over chaos, feels optimistic or hopeless."[12]

---

[12] Deepak Chopra, *The Book of Secrets*, p. 29 (Harmony Books 2004).

You could walk into these areas of a stranger's home and immediately tell a lot about that person - from the décor style to pictures on the wall to the orderliness, or lack thereof. If someone were to walk into your house, how well would they size you up? They would probably have a pretty good idea of your personality, genre of occupation, and general demographics. Simply by looking around your home, someone would have a pretty good idea of a day in the life of being you. It is the most reflective of our personality.

Because the main floor represents our present consciousness, it should have optimal energy flow. If the energy is obstructed, then you may find yourself running into blocks throughout your day. Obstructions can include such things as a bad floor plan, poor furniture arrangement, or stuff that just needs to be put away, or let go. A floor plan where rooms easily flow into each other is ideal. Even if your floor plan has a good flow, you want to make sure your furniture is not disrupting it. To check the flow of your living space, walk continuously through it as if you were the wind or energy coming through the front door. See what type of pattern you make and if you have to awkwardly change your direction due to walls, narrow hallways, furniture or any other décor items in the way.

Also notice if there are areas or even entire rooms within your living space that are rarely, if ever, utilized. If so, this is an aspect of yourself that you are underutilizing. All parts of your home should be accessible and useable. Just like your body, each and every part should be in full working condition. Otherwise, there is a block cutting off the oxygen, or energy flow, to that area.

Mind Body Home Connection: Main Level

- What is the typical state of the your main living spaces? Clean or cluttered?
- Do my main living spaces represent or express my personality?
- Do I like being in my space?

- Am I embarrassed, proud, or indifferent of others seeing my space?
- Is there too much furniture to where it's difficult to move around?
- Do my living spaces seem too sparse in need of furniture or décor items?
- Do I love every item in my space? Are there items I no longer love or use and can get rid of?

2ND Floor

As we climb upstairs, we step into our higher states of consciousness. In multi-story homes, the bedrooms are usually located on the second level, while the more public spaces are on the main level. In this case, the floors separate active, daily living from relaxing, private living. This is a great arrangement that helps set clear boundaries between active and relaxing spaces and also between public and private spaces.

Having bedrooms located on a separate floor from the everyday activity of the home will promote restful sleep. The active energy stays in the public spaces, not in the bedroom. In feng shui terms, the active spaces would be considered *yang* in nature, while the quieter, more relaxing spaces would be considered more *yin*. Because the second floor of the home is logistically less accessible to the public, we can express our private side more freely – whether that is sleeping, getting dressed, making love, dreaming, or even meditating. These are activities that are more in tune with our higher levels of consciousness. When we dream, we are accessing our subconscious mind, but also communing with our higher self and perhaps even traveling into other realms.

For those who live in a single-story home or loft-type space with no second floor, then the bedroom(s) would be the closest equivalent to a separate space. In such cases, it is best to create adequate boundaries between the public and private spaces. For typical single-story homes, this is usually accomplished with a hallway leading to the bedroom spaces. However, for an open loft or condo space this may be more challenging. Nevertheless, it is important. Try separating the space by using a different wall color for the bedroom, an area rug, or window dressing to slow the energy down to create a more yin environment.

Where Should Your Home Office Be Located?

With so many transitions in the workplace, more and more people are working from home. Unless it is a newer home, home offices usually take the form of a converted bedroom. A home-based business taking space on the second level has a different energy than one on the main level (and especially in the basement).

Offices located on the main level are more accessible to the public and therefore have more yang energy. Home offices located on upper floors are more introspective and work better for writing, healing, or creative-based businesses. Whether an office is located toward the front of the house or back of the house is also a consideration.

A home office toward the front of the home will lend to a business being more extroverted and seen in the world; whereas a home office located toward the back of the home will be more inward and yin in nature. In homes where my office was on the second floor or in the back of the home, I preferred working at coffee shops because a more yang environment better suits my energy for working.

Setting up a home office in the basement should only be used as a last resort. There is a subconscious correlation between being situated higher up and feeling important. The penthouse apartment is a classic example, as is sitting in the "catbird's seat." An office in the basement will lend to feelings of inadequacy. It will also be difficult to move the business forward. It may bring up insecurities that stem from childhood that negatively affecting work performance, not to mention health considerations.

I often come across male clients who have their home office in the basement. They seem not to mind it, until I start asking them questions. In one case, my client, Tom, said he loved working in the basement due to its privacy. He then mentioned suffering from headaches on a daily basis. It was no wonder since the space had no natural light, only fluorescent lighting.

Situating your office on the main floor or higher will give your work or business the priority and importance it needs to survive and thrive.

Attic

When I think about the energy of attic spaces, I can't help but think of Chevy Chase in *Christmas Vacation*. Because Chevy Chase's character was accidentally locked in the attic, he spent the day watching old family movies stored away in an old trunk wearing his mother's clothes to stay warm. This is indicative of the energy of attics. It almost always involves our relationship with our ancestral family members and the belief systems accompanying them.

Because the attic is the highest floor of the house, it symbolizes our higher consciousness, specifically our spirituality and connection to our higher Self. The attic is related to our 7th chakra, which connects us with the Divine, Source, or God. While the basement represents our subconscious, the attic represents our superconscious. The attic is the container for those thoughts and beliefs hindering you from expanding your horizons and reaching your highest potential. Such hindrances are usually rooted in family patterns that have been handed down over generations. Not coincidentally, both the basement and attic are areas where we store items from the past and may even interchange the items we store in those areas.

The attic is a common dream symbol. In a typical attic dream, the dreamer may be observing old items in the attic or family members may appear in the attic with us. You may have had a dream at some point of being in an attic. If so, it was most likely at a time when you were re-evaluating your beliefs or spirituality. Perhaps you were breaking the mold within your family ancestral roots. At some point in our life, we usually start to question the beliefs that were passed down to us. We make a determination as to whether certain beliefs are still in alignment with us, or not. They could be rooted from childhood, societal standards, or even our ancestral DNA.

Items stored in the attic may be directly related to a family connection in the case of inherited items or family photos and memorabilia. Or the attic may contain items with no direct family relation, but instead represent belief systems or patterns passed down. An example is Christmas décor, which is commonly stored in the attic. Christmas decorations are a symbol of a deeply rooted belief system, not to mention a 2000-year old religion. A few years ago, I contemplated whether I really wanted to have a Christmas tree at Christmas. Growing up in the Bible Belt, it was customary to go through the motions of putting up a Christmas tree and celebrating Christmas every year. Once I made the conscious choice to have a tree, it no longer seemed like a hassle or an over-imposing tradition. The power is in the conscious choice and awareness of what and why you are storing certain items.

Even if items stored in your attic do not have a familial or spiritual connotation, those items may still be blocking you in some way. Think of items stored in the attic as weight bearing down on you. Those items are a heavy energy that can weigh on you to the point of causing headaches, breathing issues, or feelings of claustrophobia. If you have storage space in your attic, take inventory of what you have stored. Notice how it differs from the stuff stored in your basement or other areas of your home.

It is not uncommon for people who have experienced paranormal activity in their home to have it come from the attic space. I have worked with several clients with this scenario. It is not coincidental that in all cases they had items stored from their past that they were unnecessarily hanging onto. Areas with stagnant energy attract more stagnant energy.

If you have ever lived in or had a bedroom in a built-out attic space, you most definitely experienced a spiritual transformation while living there, or a deepening of your spirituality. With only a six-inch deep roof between you and the heavens, your dreams may take on a different quality. For anyone who already tends to be a little spacey or need more grounding, it is not advisable to sleep or work in an attic space.

Mind Body Home Connection: Attic

- Does your home have an attic? Did your previous home have an attic?
- Do you know what is in your attic?
- What types of items do you store in your attic? Why did you choose the attic as opposed to other storage areas to store those particular items?
- Are there items stored in your attic that you no longer want or need?
- What feeling do you get when you access your attic?
- How easy or difficult is it to access your attic?
- Did your childhood home have an attic and, if so, was it used to store items?

CHAPTER 9

STRUCTURAL COMPONENTS - THE BONES OF THE HOME

Follow your bliss and the Universe will open doors where there were only walls.

—Joseph Campbell

- Framework
- Flooring
- Ceiling
- Roof
- Walls
- Fireplace
- Stairs
- Windows
- Doors

The structural components of a house are the 'bones' or 'skeletal' structure of the house. Structural components of a home would include the framing, walls, doors, windows, ceiling, and other aspects that give structure to the house. Our own physical skeletal system is the architecture that houses, or gives support to, our organ systems. Our bones, in conjunction with muscles, tendons, and ligaments, keep us upright, sturdy, and solid. And so is the case with the structural component of a house that hold the space for the individual rooms, which are akin to our organs as discussed in the next chapter.

Framework

The framework of most homes is made of wood, called "stick" construction, although some homes may be made of steel, concrete, or adobe. Like our own bones, it is important to have a strong, sturdy framework. The frame must also be conducive to its environment. Just as different cultures have different body structures depending on the weather conditions of a region, so do our homes. For example, an adobe framework would not work well in the southeast because of moisture issues. Likewise, a wood-framed house in the southwest would not make sense due to limited access to wood and the inefficiencies in cooling and heating.

Areas prone to earthquakes or hurricanes must use stronger framing than areas with less severe conditions. Usually framing materials are standard within a region for this reason. Homeowners generally don't think too much about framing, unless they are specifically drawn to a particular aesthetic finish. However, when a problem arises within the framework, it is usually a major problem and in severe cases can threaten the integrity of the entire structure. The issue can be sudden as the case of a tornado. Or it can be an issue that slowly eats away at the home, such as unknown water leak or termite infestation.

The framing of a house is representative of our bones with the drywall and other connecting and supporting components being the muscles, tendons, and ligaments. From a mind-body perspective, our bones represent our major belief systems. When someone breaks a bone, there has most likely been, or going to be, a major shift in one's life. Belief systems, or perspectives, come to the surface to be examined. A bone break or fracture could also represent a major misalignment also causing one to take a closer look at their life. It is not coincidental that such an incident causes one to slow down physically, especially in the case of a foot, ankle, or leg injury. As a result, they are forced to remove themselves from their ordinary patterns and routines, slow down, and look within.

An 'injury' to a home's framework brings up similar issues. In the case of a slow deterioration of the framing, signs eventually rear their head in the form of hairline cracks in the drywall. As the framing loses support, all that is attached weakens. To remedy the problem, usually the wall is cut into and the insides exposed. What you see is often ugly as it has been ignored for too long. It is most likely that anyone who has dealt with problems with their home's framework also underwent their own internal shifts. Instead of manifesting as an injury in the body, a structural problem shows up in the home. Either way, it calls up similar themes in one's life.

Problems with the framework of a home can also relate to not feeling supported in life. My client, Andrea, was renting her home out during the housing market crash in order to purchase another home in a desired location. She rented the home with ease and rarely, if ever, heard from her tenant receiving the rent on time each month. Toward the end of the tenancy, Andrea went inside to check on a lighting issue the tenant reported. When she walked in, she was appalled to see an entire wall not only cracked, but deep cavernous patterns entrenched in the drywall from sustained water damage.

Although she was not currently living in the home, her energy was still a part of this space as she had renovated and lived there for many years. In fact, parts of our energy remains with our homes that we have had a connection with for years, if not lifetimes, following the time we actually lived there. It's as though we leave a part of ourselves in the space, perhaps our DNA is implanted in the space. As the home undergoes transformations, we do as well.

In the case of Andrea's home, both her issues and that of her tenants manifested as a deteriorated wall. Her tenant was clearly living "in the dark" with his head in the sand to the point he didn't even notice the Grand Canyon-like valleys in the wall, partially because the light in that area had stopped working. Meanwhile, Andrea was dealing with her own issues that manifested in this 1930's bungalow. It was at a time when she was overwhelmed with the finances of owning two homes and overall felt *unsupported*. It was also not coincidental that the force that weakened and rotted the framing of the wall was water. Water is representative of our emotions. Anytime it shows up in our home in the form of a leak, or other problem, it represents our repressed or unexpressed emotions.

Mind Body Home Connection: Framework

- Do you feel supported in your life or have adequate support systems in place?
- Are big issues coming to the surface that you have been ignoring?
- Do you feel physically weak, particularly in the legs or hips?
- Is there something that is emotionally eating away at you?
- What are you ignoring in your life?
- Where are you out of alignment in your life?
- What aspect of your life do you need to take a closer look at?
- What belief systems are currently being challenged for you?

Flooring

The different levels of the home were discussed in the previous chapters, but the flooring material is also worth mentioning. The actual flooring of a space represents the division between the levels of consciousness. Having solid flooring can help create clear boundaries. If you've ever lived in an apartment with someone living above you or below you, then you know how important this division is. When you hear footsteps or music above you, it feels like a boundary has been crossed.

In the case of a house, holes or cracks in the flooring is representative of energy leaks in your life. It is not uncommon in old homes with hardwood floors to have holes or cracks that have developed over time, particularly around the baseboards. Usually there is no subflooring with only one level of plank wood between the main floor and the basement or crawl space. Even small openings make a home vulnerable to unwanted air leaks or in worse cases, bugs and rodents. This is literally and figuratively represented of energy leaks within the homeowners. It is important to fill in these openings. Also consider where in your life you are letting your energy escape, or allowing your boundary to be crossed?

To ensure proper grounding, make sure your flooring is in good condition. For example, if you have carpet, is the padding underneath in good condition, or rotted away? How many layers of linoleum are you living on in the kitchen? Or what condition is the subflooring under the tile in your bathroom? The tile may be nice and durable, but what about what the tile is sitting on? Hardwood floors are a nice option because there is nothing hidden underneath them. They are made of natural material and will withstand wear and tear.

Consider what condition your flooring is in and if it needs repair or improving. Also simply sweeping, mopping, or vacuuming your floor can be an effective grounding exercise. I find that when I start to get too in my head, I instinctively grab the Swiffer and start sweeping the floor. By simply taking my awareness to the ground and my feet, I feel more grounded.

Ceiling

Ceilings represent our perceived limits or perspectives. It's no wonder why tall ceilings feel expansive. In spaces with lofty, tall ceilings, it may feel like the "the sky is the limit." For some, this perception may be a bit overwhelming or even lack a coziness that is often desired in a space. Spaces with lower ceilings have a cozier feel lending to occupants feeling safe and protected. Lower ceilings also give the perception that life is under control with attainable goals. Depending on one's personality, however, lower ceilings could cause one to feel claustrophobic, limited, or restricted in their life.

Striking a balance between a sense of expansion and the feeling of protectiveness is ideal. This can be accomplished by differing the ceiling heights, or at least the perceived ceiling heights, within a space. I was recently in a condo space with soaring 20' ceilings with windows and skylights galore. It was an inspiring space that felt like anything was possible. This could feel overwhelming day in and day out to some. The space was perfectly paired with a separate, cozy room with a low ceiling perfect for watching movies or reading books.

There is a time to draw our energy in and a time to spread our wings. Ideally, our home should allow for both of these. Balance is key. To add expansion to a low-ceiling room, add lighting, preferably natural lighting. To make an expansive room feel more cozy, lower the lighting either with window shades or dimmed lighting. Feeling grounded paired with the ability to soar is the perfect balance. For businesses, adjusting ceiling heights to correlate with their mission is also advisable.

Ceilings are generally problem-free with the exception of water leaks. A leak usually originates from the roof or an upstairs bathroom or plumbing area resulting in water damage to the ceiling. In decoding what the message your home is communicating, consider from what room the leak originated. Water represents emotions and when it presents itself as a leak it means we are undergoing emotions of which we are not consciously aware. Because the ceiling represents our limitations or perspectives, then certain limitations are affecting you on an emotional level of which you are not aware. In this case, consider whether you need to make an adjustment in your life.

Mind Body Home Connection: Ceiling

- Have you reached your "glass ceiling"?
- Do you feel like you can adequately spread your wings?

- Are you feeling limited?
- Is there a new perspective that would benefit you?
- Have you created so much safety around you to the point of feeling stagnant?
- Do you feel stifled in your relationship(s) or job?
- Do you feel the "sky's the limit" or blocked?

Roof

The roof is the exterior barrier of the home that protects us from the forces of nature. It is also the point of connection between the physical world and the spiritual world. When the roof is damaged, we become vulnerable to external influences. If the damage comes in the form of a water leak, then it is on the emotional level. It could be unexpressed emotions triggered from annoyances or unwanted influences in your life. In the case of a limb or tree puncturing through the roof, then this could signify a puncture in one's deeply rooted spiritual beliefs. In the case of rain coming through the roof, the occupants are receiving a forced cleansing in which new ideas pour down like rain washing away old habits.

If the roof is falling in due to neglect, decay, or other damage, this may indicate that expectations are not measuring up or a loss of hope in some aspect of yourself. Perhaps you've given up in life, or God has let you down in some way. Once fixed, however, that aspect of yourself has the opportunity for transformation and healing. Also, taking the time to fix something before it becomes an emergency situation is the same as preventative medicine. For example, repair the roof before it starts leaking. In doing so, you are being proactive in protecting yourself so that you don't reach the point of feeling vulnerable to externals.

The roof also relates to our 7th chakra and symbolic of our connection with our higher self, spirituality, and/or God. As you experience changes with your roof, you will also have new insights, perspectives, or beliefs relating to spirituality. When you get a new roof on your home as a result of damage or general wear and tear, it can mark a shift in one's belief system with regard to religion and/or spirituality.

Mind Body Connection: Roof

- Have you had a shift in your beliefs about spirituality?
- Have you experienced a disappointment for which you had high expectations?
- Do you feel vulnerable or unsafe in the world?
- Do you struggle with setting boundaries?
- Is there a belief system you are still holding on to that no longer serves you?

Walls

The walls within a space are the main dictator of how energy flows through a space. How the energy flows through your home is indicative of how energy flows through you, physically and mentally. Walls represent boundaries. They can also signify our limitations and obstacles. Removing walls has become an increasingly common renovation project, particularly for those living in older homes. It is no wonder. As we evolve, we break through so many limiting thoughts and beliefs.

Generally speaking, the older a home, the more walls it has. My 1920s bungalow had a lovely, open floor plan that easily flowed around a central staircase. However, this was the case only because multiple doors were completely removed thereby allowing the rooms to flow and the energy meander. Older floor plans were designed to be more compartmentalized. Rooms had more defined functions sometimes even based on gender and class.

As we as a society have broken through these molds, our floor plans reflect this change. No longer do we have servants who work in the basement kitchen. And no longer do men have a smoking parlor.

(Although, they may still have a "man cave".) Generally speaking, the newer a home, the fewer walls it has. Open floor plans have not become just a trend, but a way of life. A home with an open floor plan feels lighter and freer. Breathing is easier.

Loft apartments have the fewest walls with exception of the bathroom and maybe a bedroom. Not coincidentally, lofts are located in open-minded areas within a city and generally occupied by those of a similar mindset. For some people, the openness can feel too overwhelming and scary with too many options. A more closed floor plan may be desired by someone in order to feel more in control of their surroundings and life.

If you are renovating your home and taking down a wall, think about what limitations you are currently overcoming in your life. Is there a wall in your home that you have considered removing to open up your floor plan? If so, it may reflect a desire to open up in your life and break through old habits, beliefs, or way of thinking. Open a wall and you will open your mind.

On the contrary, have you put up or wanted to put up a wall to add more division or privacy within your home? This is not as common, unless you are reconstructing the floor plan and moving rooms around. Consider where in your life you are setting new boundaries. Or is there an overall change in your way of thinking that is shifting in many rooms, or areas, of your life. A client of mine completely renovated their home after she and her husband remarried. She intuitively knew that there needed to be a shift in the space. Rooms were rearranged; walls came down; and new ones were put up.

Every house has at least one load-bearing wall. This wall is essential to the entire structure of the house and should never be removed. The load-bearing wall represents a foundational belief. What is the load-bearing wall in your life? In rare cases, a natural disaster may force you to rebuild a wall. This would be equivalent to a freak accident causing an injury to the body. Like a broken bone that is rebuilt, the wall will be stronger than before.

***Mind Body Home Connection:* Walls**
- What is blocking you creatively?
- Where are you putting up walls in your life?
- Are you too open-minded or closed-minded?
- Do you tend to be too tunnel-visioned?
- How are you with setting boundaries? Too loose or rigid?
- Does your breath flow easily through your body or is it stuck or strained?
- Do you feel like you are going up against obstacles or hitting a wall?

Fireplace

The fireplace symbolizes family, warmth, and traditional values. The fireplace has been a central focus of homes for centuries -- a place where families have traditionally gathered. Stockings are hung on the fireplace, along with family heirlooms placed on the mantle and family pictures hung above it. The fireplace is almost always the focal point of any room in which it is located. In cases of natural disasters such as a tornado, the fireplace is often the only part of the home still standing. It provides grounding for the entire home. It gives a home the feeling of safety, dependability, and warmth. That being said, if not properly utilized it can be a source of energy escaping. The chimney flue is a common area that allows energy to escape and/or unwanted energy to enter the home.

Stairs

The general shape of a house can create an underlying energy pattern for the home and its occupants. Single-story homes allow its inhabitants to work on the here and the now in the present moment of their daily life, while those in a multi-story home have the opportunity to embark on a journey to higher awareness. Neither path is better than the other as we all end up in the home that best fits our path.

Inherent to multi-story homes is a staircase. While we think of going *down* the stairs to the basement, we think of going *up* the stairs to reach the upper floors with the main level being the point of reference. Walking up a flight of stairs indicates ascension. Stairs or elevators are common dream symbols that represent making progress on one's spiritual journey. Going up stairs or elevators is like ascending to new heights; whereas going down the stairs represents descending into the subconscious mind.

It is important that stairs and stairwells be kept in good working order. You don't want anything tripping you up on your journey or getting in your way. Tripping up the stairs can signify that you are getting tripped up on your journey, most likely out of fear and self-sabotage. Keep stairs clear of clutter and fix any boards that are loose. Have a steady stair rail along the staircase so that you can feel supported as well.

Stairways can pose some issues in feng shui. Stairs can create a tunnel of rushing energy depending on where they are situated. One of the most well-known feng shui rules is that you don't want your front door to open up to a staircase. This is the case because the energy rushes up the stairs from the front door. The energy should instead meander through the main level of the home. The energy also runs down the stairs and out the front door. In terms of energy, think of stairs as an Olympic luge slide with energy rushing down.

If you have a staircase in your home, notice where it falls on the Bagua Map in Chapter 4. If that area is a challenging aspect in your life, then it is advisable to ground the energy around the staircase. Plants can be used at the bottom of the staircase to help ground the space. Placing or hanging a crystal around or above the staircase can also be used to balance the energy. Because stairs are transitional in nature, they can cause a great deal of transition in certain areas of your life depending on their location. It is also best to avoid a spiral staircase. The energy of a spiral staircase mirrors that of a corkscrew and can wreak havoc on the energy of its occupants, potentially causing health problems.

Windows

Windows are one of the most sought out aspects of a home. When I ask clients where their favorite room or part of the house is, almost inevitably everyone points to a spot where there is a window with natural light pouring in. We are naturally drawn to the outdoors. Feeling the comforts of home while feeling the connection with nature or the outside world is the balance to which most of us are drawn. Windows provide this connection.

If the house were a body, then the windows would be the eyes. The eyes are the "windows to the soul." By looking in someone's eyes, you can immediately drop into their soul. It is a similar analogy with regard to someone looking through the windows of our home. If it is someone we don't know, we feel violated, rightfully so, as they are peering into a very private space - our home, our soul.

Looking out through our eyes or windows opens us up and connects us with the outside world. With our eyes closed, we can go inward. With our eyes open, our energy naturally extends outward into the world. So is the case with our windows at home. Windows represent new perspectives, possibilities, and insights. If you need a new perspective or clarity in your life, then clean your windows. You will be amazed at how much better you can "see" your life and new possibilities. Things that were under your nose and you were unable to see will magically be revealed.

Windows also symbolize our outlook on life, point of view, and intuition. Like the eyes looking out into the world, how well can you see? Perhaps you need more clarity. Are you looking through smudged glasses, rose-colored glasses, or clear glasses? In the case of a broken window, what are you not seeing clearly? What is distorting your perception? Do you need a new point of view? Are your windows always covered up to where you are avoiding the outside world? Or why do you not want to be "seen" by the world? On the contrary, are you completely exposed and in need of boundaries? Are you open to others' point of view or just from your narrow vantage point? In the event of a broken window, what are you not seeing that is trying to get your attention?

Mind Body Home Connection: **Windows**

- Do you need more clarity on a certain area in your life?
- What are you unwilling to look at?
- What are you in denial about?
- Do you need a new perspective or viewpoint on a particular matter?

Doors

Doors represent opportunities. There are many phrases and quotes that relate to doors and how they relate to opportunities. We even use the two words synonymously in common clichés, for example, "Waiting for the right door to open." Doors can also represent entering a new stage in life or a new beginning. Doors can also represent a fork in the road of available choices we have in life, for example, choosing "Door #1 or Door #2."

In feng shui, the front door of the home is called the *primary mouth of chi*. The front door is the main vessel of energy that comes into your home and therefore the most important door for allowing new opportunities and possibilities to come into your life. For this reason, it is best to create a welcoming entrance in order to invite new opportunities into your life. Clear out any dirt or cobwebs in that area.

Make sure the front entrance is clearly marked with house numbers, a welcome mat, a door knocker or doorbell, and any other adornments that bring in positive energy. Hinges should be fully operational. Do not block any doorways with furniture or clutter. A doorbell or door knocker represents messages. The phrase, "when opportunity comes knocking," is a common metaphor that exemplifies the symbolism. If you have a doorbell, make sure it works properly so that you don't miss out on the opportunities when they do come your way. If you don't have a doorbell, then a door knocker will serve the same purpose.

Even if you don't use your front door as your main entrance it is nonetheless the primary path of energy into your home. It is therefore important to keep the energy welcoming and flowing through this area.

If you enter your home through the garage or back door, then use your front door as often as possible for getting the mail, taking a walk, or simply opening up for fresh air. Think of the front door as the inhalation or in-breath of the home with the back door being the exhalation or out-breath. It is important to keep this flow for a complete balance of the home's energy.

When I visit clients' homes that primarily use the garage or back door as their main entrance, I typically find the area around the front door to be a ghost town of sorts. The foyer area is completely ignored and the energy is stagnant. They are usually lacking energy themselves. No area of the home should go ignored, especially the front door. Add some plants to the front porch or your favorite piece of art in the front foyer. Bring some energy to that area and see what opportunities come your way.

The same is true for all doors and doorways in your home. While the front door is the primary mouth of chi, all doors allow energy to pass through and represent opportunities or openings in our life. All doors should open up fully into a room without bumping into furniture or other hindrances. Avoid storing items behind doors. The area behind doors should not be used for storage beyond that of a single robe or coat hook. I often have clients who try to use this space to hide clutter that they don't know what to do with. When a door cannot fully open, it creates a block somewhere in your life.

Doors that don't properly close indicate a misalignment in some area of your life. This could result from a framing or foundation issue that caused the floor to shift. Doors should open and close with ease. Any catches that prevent this should be remedied to avoid a "rubbing" up against things in your life. Doors with too much space or gaps should also be fixed with weather stripping otherwise this could lead to boundary issues in the form of allowing energy to escape. When energy in the form of utilities escapes so does your personal energy.

The **key lock** is another component of a door that is laced with symbolism. Usually this pertains to the front door, but it could apply to any doors with locks. Problems unlocking a door or getting a key stuck indicates anxiety pertaining to a situation occurring within the home. It's as if you subconsciously don't want to come home due to a situation within the home.

The **doorknob** holds significance as well. It is the resource you need to make necessary connections. In other words, the door and the opportunities it brings are useless without the doorknob. Problems with doorknobs or door handles indicate whether you have a "handle" on things in your life. Or, does life seem out of control to the point where you need to "get a handle on things" or "get a grip?"

Have you ever turned a doorknob to find it in your hand? When I moved into my home, the renovators had put a cheap doorknob on a beautiful 1900's door. The knob didn't fit the door properly and was always loose, to the point where it would come off in your hand when opening the door. I replaced it with a beautiful, vintage, solid brass knob. What a difference it made entering the house. There was a renewed confidence in stepping through the threshold and into the home that set a positive tone each time I entered.

Mind Body Home Connection: Doors

- Are you blocking opportunities that are coming your way?
- Are you open to new opportunities or is fear getting in the way?
- Are you fearful of change?
- Do you feel closed off from the world?
- Are you overwhelmed with choices being presented?

CHAPTER 10

ROOMS: OUR MANY PARTS AND PERSONAS

I think when you invite people to your home,
you invite them to yourself

- Oprah Winfrey

- Bathroom
- Bedroom
- Closet
- Den (or Living Room)
- Garage
- Transitional Spaces
- Kitchen

You're walking through your home, down a hall, and you notice a door. For some reason you've never noticed this door before and decide to open it. You step through and discover a part of your home that you never knew existed. You can't figure out why you've never known of this room or perhaps even an entire wing of the house until now.

You walk through with eyes wide open. The room may feel spacious and open. Or perhaps it has a unique characteristic about it. Maybe it is a room with a giant piano in it, a stage, or some other message. This is a common dream scenario in which you are discovering a new aspect of yourself - a new room. While it's been with you all along, you are just now noticing it.

As we grow, expand, and evolve, we reclaim parts of ourselves that we may have abandoned long ago. We pull back parts of ourselves like a superhero taking back his or her superpowers. Perhaps it is a talent in music, speaking, or the arts that you denied. As we become more of ourself, we add tools to our toolbox. These new aspects could come through a new relationship with someone who awakens something within. It could be an entire new career path or skill set. Each room of the house represents an aspect of ourself, or our psyche, in some way.

This is also the case on a more literal level in our waking life as well. As we build an addition to our home, we are adding a new aspect of ourself. As we move into a larger home with more rooms, we have the opportunity to access new aspects of ourself. However, the abruptness can sometimes be too much and take time to integrate the expansion. Moving to a smaller space may give you the opportunity to hone in and focus on more specifics aspects of one's self. Think of it as a recalibration of one's essential self of what is truly important.

In spaces with fewer rooms, such as a loft apartment or dorm room, life is not as compartmentalized. As a result, the lines may blur as to the functions of the room. While this may be liberating at times, it can also be confusing. Functions become mixed as you eat on the bed, work on the couch, and sleep in your living room. Creating divisions of space is helpful in creating "rooms" energetically. Rugs make great dividers. Curtain dividers can be added and furniture can be arranged to create a division of space, thereby creating rooms without walls.

Rooms are individualized spaces that are inherently compartmentalized. Similar to our brain, certain areas of our home are responsible for certain tasks or ways of thinking and operating. For example, the bedroom is for sleeping; the bathroom is for cleansing; the kitchen is for nurturing, and so forth. Each of these functions represents a certain aspect of ourselves that is essential to us being whole.

Let's take a look at the most common rooms and what each represents. In doing so, consider the representation of each room in tandem with the other sections in Part II. Think of the rooms as the stage on which the other messages play out. For example, if you have a water leak, in which room does it show up? If there is a faulty door, into which room does it lead? For any ancillary repair or maintenance that arises in your home, in which room does it reveal itself. This will indicate to which area of your life the message is pertaining.

Bathroom

The bathroom is the room that naturally requires the most privacy. Not coincidentally, the bathroom is a common dream symbol relating to exposure. Almost everyone has had a dream where they are in the bathroom with the door open representing exposure of something in your life that is private to you. In feng shui, the bathroom is considered to be an inauspicious room. Because water represents money in feng shui, the draining and flushing facilities in a bathroom wash benevolent chi out of the home. Hence, the phrase, "flushing money down the drain."

In our collective consciousness, the bathroom most directly relates to letting go, releasing, and detoxifying. Before modern plumbing was introduced, toilets were located outside the home in an outhouse so that the toxins would not infiltrate the fresh water. Since then, the function of the bathroom has evolved. Now bathrooms can be an elaborate, spa-like setting with renewal, purification, and self-care being the focus. In effect, there is a constant renewal process that takes place in the bathroom with each step being as important as the other. As important as it is to cleanse ourselves, it is equally important to take care and even pamper ourselves.

The primary theme of a bathroom is water. Without water a bathroom clearly has no function. It is water that drains, flows, flushes, cleans, and rinses us. **Water** represents emotions. Water is a common dream symbol that shows up in a myriad of ways in our dreams - a boat, a wave, an ocean, a lake, a leak, a river, a canoe. Regardless, it relates to emotions that have not reached the conscious level. The state of the water is always significant in determining the level or quality of emotion being experienced.

When unconscious emotions are manifested through the home, they often show up in plumbing problems. Plumbing will be discussed in more detail in Chapter 11 and should be considered in tandem with this section. When plumbing problems arise in the bathroom, it generally relates to difficulties in releasing and expressing one's emotions. This is particularly the case with problems relating to the toilet. The **toilet** represents that which we don't want anyone else knowing about or being exposed to. It can also relate to anything toxic in our life that needs to be purged or released, but continues to hang on, such as toxic relationships, toxic diet, or toxic habits.

The **toilet seat** is an integral component of a toilet and represents taking a seat or taking the time in which to release toxic emotions. At the time I owned two homes simultaneously, I had to replace three toilet seats within a couple of weeks. Before that, I had never purchased a toilet seat. After going to the hardware store for the third time for a toilet seat, I realized there was a deeper meaning. I was so busy with everything that had to be done in a short amount of time that I wasn't taking the time to release my emotions.

The **toilet handle** or flusher is a common plumbing repair. Similar to the doorknob on a door, it facilitates the act of flushing. When in disrepair, it represents hesitancy or fear in releasing emotions.

Also consider the bathroom fixtures that relate to cleansing in general, such as the **shower**, **sink**, and **bathtub**. With these, the flow of water is more steady and gentler and therefore relates to the daily cleansing of emotions necessary to maintain a healthy balance. When these fixtures are in need of repair, then self-care should be considered. Are you taking care of yourself? Are you crying out for more self-care, more alone time, or outlets for release?

Bedroom

The bedroom signifies the most intimate aspects of ourselves. It is the personal sanctuary of the home where we sleep, dream, make love, and transcend the physical plane. Second only to a meditation or prayer room, it connects us with the spiritual realm. The bedroom is an intimate space that we generally keep private. When entertaining, we often close the door to this room to maintain our sense of privacy or redirect traffic accordingly.

The bedroom should only contain those items related to sleep, relaxation, and intimacy. By no means should you have exercise equipment in the bedroom. The bedroom should maintain a quiet, yin energy conducive to relaxation, sleeping, and rejuvenation. Keep books and other energetic objects to a minimum. Look around your bedroom and notice what you are having a relationship with. Is it the TV, computer, your children (photos), or your books?

In my observations as a feng shui consultant, people often unconsciously set up blocks or barriers in their bedroom to ward off intimate relationships. For couples with marital issues, disharmony is always reflected in their bedroom. For chronically single people, the block can always be found in their bedroom as well. Here's how to avoid those pitfalls and instead amp things up in your love life.

Nightstands – Nothing tells me more about the state of a relationship than the nightstands. I have had couples' relationships shift dramatically simply by changing or adding nightstands. It represents the equality (or lack thereof) in the relationship. It is important to have a nightstand on each side of the bed. Secondly, you want the nightstands to be of equal weight. While they don't have to match, they need to be approximately the same height and density. Third, the lamps on the nightstands should also be of the same height and density. In other words, you don't want a tall lamp on one side and a small reader clip on the other. Of course, this speaks to aesthetics as well.

Even Numbers – Numbers are our oldest symbols and therefore very impressionable to our collective subconscious mind. For that reason, it is important to have objects placed in pairs. If you have a candle in the room, make it two. If you have pillows on the bed, make it two, four, or six. Resist the urge to have that single decorative pillow beaming out at you each night as you pull the covers down. You want to avoid the *number one*, even including items that are shaped like the number one. I was recently in a client's bedroom where there was a picture of a single, lonely bird and a tall decorative candle sconce that looked like a gigantic number one across from her bed. For couples, avoid the *number three* to avoid a third party entering the relationship. These numbers could show up in artwork, accessories, or bedding.

Mirrors – Speaking of threes, do not place a mirror across from the bed as it is said to bring a third party into the relationship. If you are single, you could be brought into a triangulated relationship that is not of your choosing. If you requre a mirror in the bedroom, have it on a sidewall, or better yet, inside a closet door. Mirrors generate a lot of energy and can also interfere with quality sleep.

Paint Colors – Stick with warm, calming, and relaxing colors. This could vary depending on one's personality. Some ideas for paint colors include chocolate, burgundy, dark or light neutrals, a meditative deep blue or plum. You want a color that blends well with skin tones and promotes a good night's sleep. Colors emits energy, so avoid bright yellows, reds, and other primary colors.

Bedding – Invest in new bedding and sheets. Go for tactile and texture. Romance is all about the physical pleasures in life. Make your bedding a feast for the senses. Ditch the comforter that you've had since college or the one with dog hair all over it. Get some new, clean sheets; a warm cozy, fuzzy blanket; and a comforter or duvet that you could lose yourself in. Add some pillows with varying textures for effect.

Checklist: What to Do and Not to Do in the Bedroom for Love

- *Don't* have a teddy bear on your bed.
- *Do* use luxurious and rich linens.
- *Don't* have only one nightstand
- *Do* have a nightstand on each side of the bed that are of equal size.
- *Don't* have one side of your bed up against the wall.
- *Do* make the bed the focal point of the room.
- *Don't* have images of single people or single animals in your bedroom.
- *Don't* have a mirror across from your bed.
- *Don't* have memorabilia or any reminder of your ex in your bedroom.
- *Do* keep notes or cards from your love in the bedroom.
- *Don't* have decor items grouped in 1's, 3's, or 5's.
- *Do* have objects grouped together in 2's or 4's, i.e. pillows, candles, etc.
- *Don't* have pictures of family members in your bedroom.
- *Do* have images of you and your loved one.
- *Don't* have trinkets, collections, furniture from your childhood in your bedroom.
- *Do* keep artwork and décor items fresh and relevant to your current life.

Closet

The closet symbolizes aspects of ourselves that we want to keep hidden. We hide "our skeletons in the closet." And, of course, there is the common phrase, "coming out of the closet," that references expressing an aspect of ourself that we have kept hidden from the world. Most everyone has hidden aspects or parts of themselves that they don't want others to see or know about. The closet is that space where we store items so that others can't see them, nor do we have to look at them ourselves. We generally have a variety of different types of closets in our homes and spaces with different organizing functions, such as a linen closet, Christmas decoration closet, or coat closet. For example, the clothing closet has a very different energy than the storage closet at the end of the hall. Consider the different functions of closets in assessing the meaning of your space.

The **clothing closet** or wardrobe is the closet that is most personal to us. It contains our identities. It contains the many "hats" we wear in life. It reflects our personality. It is also holds the most opportunity for making major changes in your life. "Cleaning out your closet" is a common metaphor relating to getting rid of things in your life that are no longer in your highest and best interest, and in doing so, it allows space for new things to come into your life. For example, I will never forget the day that I got rid of the very last business suit that I had worn as a practicing attorney. It was a huge moment for me. In the week following that, my phone rang off the hook with numerous new clients interested in my healing services.

The "catch-all" **storage closets** tend to accumulate the most clutter. We throw things in there that we don't know what to do with or deal with. For some, the need for organization and control will show up in the closet spaces. For others, it is a black hole of stuff that gets stored for years without any remembrance as to what is in there. If you don't have a basement, then closets can become the storage alternative of choice for those items. While storing items is essential and important, be conscious of what you are storing. Only store items that you love, use, or which have a purpose.

Den (or Living Room)

The den or living room represents the way in which we go through our day. It displays our personality and represents our basic beliefs. We usually display photos and art personal to us and that represents who we are. In the case of families, the den is similar to that of an animal's den where the family congregates together. It provides a space for bonding and enjoying one another's company. In today's world, the focal point of the den or living room is often the television; whereas it was once the fireplace. In the event of repairs or maintenance in this area of the home, consider the state of the family unit within the home.

Homes often have a family room separate from a living room, thereby separating family and entertainment spaces. In the case of a living room used for entertaining, the room expresses the outward personality that we present to the rest of the world. The colors and décor items should express who we are. For living room spaces used primarily for entertaining, furniture is best arranged in conversational setting. Formal living rooms have slowly faded away as our lifestyles have changed. It is rare for formal living rooms to be built into new floor plans. Instead, home offices have taken front and center in the home where the formal living room once was.

Garage

As we leave our home each morning, we transition from home and into the world through the garage. We get into our car and head to our job, chores, or other daily activities that are part of our outer purpose. Cars represent our direction, purpose, and ambition in life. Thus, the garage holds this space for us. It is the entry and exit point between home and work. Garages have become a prominent aspect of homes as the role of our cars has evolved. While historic homes have no garages at all, modern-day homes often prominently display the garage at the front of the home. With the garage at the front of the home, it is common for the occupants to place a high importance on their cars with regard to identity, status, or even as an important hobby.

Ideally, your garage should be treated with as much love and care as any other room in the house. When I remind workshop attendees that the garage is included in the Bagua Map, I usually get sighs and comments, such as "that explains it" when they realize their Love corner is buried somewhere in the corner of their garage or their Wealth is stashed away behind the inherited furniture collecting dust in the garage. The garage is as important as any room in the house. After all it is an aspect of yourself, as are all parts of your home.

Clearing out the clutter is step one. Organization is usually the key in preventing the clutter from coming back. Make the garage as welcoming as possible. After all, it is the first space you come home to. You don't want to feel overwhelmed before you even walk in the house. Consider adding a piece of art or a personal memento as you come in the door welcoming you home. The garage is your subconscious mind's first impression of your home and the state of your life. Make it a good one!

I see many garages that are so full of clutter to the point where a single car will not fit. The garage ends up being a giant storage unit. This is often the case with folks with no basement and thus the garage ends up taking on the role of the basement. If that is the case, then read the "Basement" section in Chapter 8 for more clarity as to what this section of the home means for you. If you use the garage to park your car, then make sure your car can get in and out of the garage with no problem. There should be enough space to allow the car doors to open with ease so that you can get in and out of the car. Hindrances from getting in and out of the garage or car represents blocks in your career or direction in life.

Transitional Spaces

Hallways, foyers, and corridors are transitional spaces that often get overlooked. Nonetheless, they are an important and essential energetic component of the home. Transitional spaces, including foyers, hallways, or any corridors connect one room to another. They are the opening act preceding the main attraction. They provide a pause and a build-up to the adjoining spaces.

Transitional spaces are representative of those transitional times in our lives. Transitions are inherently challenging, but necessary. It is the in-between space where there is little certainty or familiarity. If one moves into a new relationship, job, or life change too quickly, we can feel jolted and ungrounded. This is the gift of transitions and transitional spaces. Like Goldilocks, transitional spaces shouldn't be too big or too small, but just right. For example, if a hallway is too long, then it leads to energy getting stuck. If a transitional space isn't big enough, for example in the case of a foyer, then the transition is too abrupt and therefore unsettling.

Hallways are akin to veins and arteries to our heart and lungs that feed chi energy throughout the home. Hallways can directly affect the breathing patterns of its occupants. For this reason, they must be kept free of clutter and unnecessary furnishings and objects. Hallways and pass-through spaces should have at least a three-foot width with four feet being preferable. Avoid placing furniture in hallways that encroach upon a comfortable width.

Depending on their length and shape, hallways can cause energy to rush too fast or to become too stagnant. If the hallway is narrow and dark, then the energy can stall almost like a black hole. In this case, it is important to have adequate lighting. Also consider painting the walls a lighter color to bring in more yang energy. Adding a mirror in the hallway is another way to bring in more energy.

For hallways that end with a door or window at the end, it is important to slow the energy down before it reaches the end of the hallway where the energy will exit the home. Putting a shade on the window or door will help prevent the energy from escaping. Another remedy is to hang a crystal from a ceiling light in the hallway to help evenly distribute the chi flow. If the bathroom is located at the end of a hallway, keep the door closed to avoid the energy rushing down the hallway and then down the toilet.

Kitchen

The kitchen is the heart of the home. It's where the party always ends up as we have an insatiable need to be fed and nourished by its warmth. It is also the nurturing center of the home and synonymous with a nurturing mother. When you look back on your childhood and some of the most memorable times, they most likely took place in the kitchen. Whether cooking, paying bills, having morning coffee, or having important discussions, the kitchen is the hub for the home. It is therefore important that you love your kitchen.

For resell purposes, the kitchen is often considered the most important room of the house. Most real estate agents will tell you that putting money into renovating your kitchen is the best investment you can make in improving your home. Whether renovating or making small changes to your kitchen, you are nourishing yourself in the process. It is the space most directly related to our overall health and wellbeing. If you are suffering from an illness, pay particular importance to the state of your kitchen. It is a reflection of your health and how you are taking care of yourself. If you are not well enough, then have a loved one or someone else clean the kitchen, keep foods fresh on hand, and even add fresh flowers.

In feng shui, the most powerful component of the home is the stove. The **stove** is representative of your personal energy or power. It is a strong fire element and related to your own inner flame that burns brightly within you. Be conscious to use all burners on your stove equally. We all have our favorite ones that we gravitate toward, but in doing so you are underutilizing all of your power. Keep your stove clean. Also fix any burners that are not working properly to have all of your personal power accessible.

CHAPTER 11

MECHANICALS: THE FUNCTIONING ORGAN SYSTEMS

Buildings, too, are children of Earth and Sun.
- Frank Lloyd Wright

- Plumbing
- Electricity
- Internet/Telephone
- Heating and Air Systems

The mechanicals of a home are those amenities that keep the home functioning with fresh water, cool air, electricity, and hot water. When one of the mechanicals isn't working properly, it can wreak havoc on the occupants. Suddenly, there is no light. No hot water for bathing. And no pilot light for cooking. It is those modern amenities that we so take for granted; that is, until we don't have them.

The mechanicals pump the blood, keep the air flowing, and help regulate our emotions. They are akin to the functioning organ systems in our body. They keep everything operating and running smoothly. Because mechanicals are operational in nature, similar to electronics, they are quite responsive to the energy of its occupants. All mechanicals go through normal wear and tear or degradation with time. However, it is when components unexpectedly or unexplainably break when one should take a closer look at the messages that lie therein. Let's take a look at the most common mechanicals in spaces and their correlating meanings.

Plumbing

Plumbing sources water into the home and sends grey or toxic water out of the home. It is the component that deals with all things water-related. Any sort of water or fluid - whether it is in the body as a tear, in your dream as a lake, or in the house as plumbing - is symbolic of emotions. With regard to plumbing, specifically, water pertains to the release of emotions.

Some homes are chronically plagued with water problems, while other homes rarely experience water issues aside from regular maintenance. One home I lived in constantly had plumbing problems. When I least expected it (usually on a Sunday), a leak would spring from one of the pipes. I lived in this house during a transitional time of life when I was learning to better connect with my emotions. By fixing plumbing leaks, an energetic opening takes place that allows you to simultaneous process the stuck emotion as well. As you make changes to your home, you will experience an emotional shift in some way yourself.

Plumbing pipes specifically deal with how we direct and control the flow of our emotions. The most common example is a **clogged pipe.** In such a case, you are most likely experiencing a clog of emotions that are not properly flowing. Also consider in which room the clog is for a more detailed interpretation. For example, a clog in the bathroom can mean a problem releasing toxic emotions, whereas a clog in the kitchen may mean you are not sharing with others those emotions closest to your heart or letting others know your needs for nurturing.

A **clogged toilet** is another common plumbing clog. It signifies that you are holding on to something(s) that you no longer need but can't seem to let go of. Not surprisingly, this is often associated with kidney problems, lower intestinal issues, diarrhea and constipation. A toilet flushes away toxins and waste that your body no longer needs. If it is clogged, then you are holding on to emotions, memories, relationships, or thought patterns no longer serving you.

What happens when the toilet becomes clogged for too long? An imbalance. The toilet begins overflowing. This correlates with when emotions get carried away and out of control due to being pent up for too long. The emotions have reached the point where they can no longer be ignored. The proper channel that the water or emotions should take is being misdirected and ends up in the floor. Now it must be dealt with once and for all.

A broken plumbing line is a dreaded occurrence that can happen as a result of either the pipe being brittle with age, wear and tear of joints, or stress from being frozen. Any of these are the result of emotions being stored and built up to the point they have nowhere else to go. The difference between this incident and the clog is that the broken pipe is usually buried deep in the ground and therefore involves a more difficult fix. Just getting to the pipe often involves digging up the ground, thereby exposing things that were buried long ago. Emotions that you really didn't want to ever look at and maybe even forgot about may resurface for healing.

One of the broken plumbing lines I experienced was underneath my aggregate concrete driveway. The water was seeping up through the cracks to let me know there was a problem below the surface. As the plumber's excavating crew was making a slice into the concrete, I knew it was a message for me. Sure enough, it was just a few days later I learned that I would need to have my own surgery to remove a cyst.

Have you ever felt numb or emotionally frozen? Depending on the season and one's geography, this can sometimes manifest into **frozen pipes**. In the South where I grew up, it's not uncommon to drip the faucets when temperatures get into the teens and single digits. Even being conscious of the potential problem and taking precautions, I have had several occasions when pipes have frozen. It's not the actual freezing that causes damage, but the thawing process. In other words, it's when the emotions begin moving again that the burst occurs. It is the abnormal expansion and contraction that causes stress on the pipes just like that of an emotional imbalance. Winter is a difficult time for many people as the trees are stripped of leaves and the ground is barren of life. It is a time in which we are forced to look within and can therefore be a challenging time to deal with emotions.

A friend of mine had an interesting experience with her pipes freezing. She was just coming out of a transitional period, temporarily living with friends. The pipes froze at the house she was housesitting and then again a week later at another house where she was staying. It is not coincidental that she was just transitioning out of a period of feeling 'stuck' in her life into a new vibrant stage of her life. Although she was going through an emotionally freezing and thawing time of her life, she was conscious of her emotional state throughout and luckily neither pipe actually burst.

A lot of us have experienced water leaks that are not from bad plumbing, but from Mother Nature. Water leaks and floods occur most commonly in roofs, walls, floors, and really just about anywhere. Throughout my entire childhood, we had a leak that came in around the chimney and down the fireplace. Like plumbing, it is a message about your emotions. To fully understand the meaning you have to consider where the leak is.

Pinpoint the location of the leak and consider the meaning of the correlating room or floor. For example, if the leak is in the ceiling of your bedroom, consider your emotional state surrounding your current romantic relationship, or lack thereof. Are you upset about a relationship or in denial? Also, refer to the Bagua Map to see what that particular room represents. For example, it may be the Career corner. Did you recently get turned down for a promotion and try to blow it off as if it didn't bother you?

When you come across the correct interpretation for you, it will resonate with you. Also, the meaning may be specific to you. For example, the leak around the fireplace where I grew up may mean emotional issues relating to a lack of warmth, tradition, and family. But, that fireplace has a more specific meaning to my family. My parents, sister and I (at age 4) hauled the stone to build the two-story fireplace from an abandoned, broken stone wall for what seemed like months during the hot summer. The hauling was a grueling task that I can still remember took blood, sweat, and probably tears. There's no telling what energy those stones held over time, not to mention the stress my parents were under in building their first home.

The **hot water heater** is a specific component of plumbing that usually requires replacing every 8-10 years. Because the hot water heater is usually located out of sight, out of mind, we often don't notice when it starts leaking and in need of replacement. This can often wreak havoc in a basement or storage area where it is kept. I have heard many stories where the water flooded important storage items or areas in the home. Energetically, this is similar to repressed emotions, but with more fire behind it. Being a unit that creates hot water means that the repressed emotions are based in anger.

Mind Body Home Connection: Plumbing

- Have you been storing up emotions?
- Do you need to have a good cry?
- What do you need to let go of?
- What are you in denial about?
- Are you experiencing issues with kidneys, liver, lower intestinal issues, diarrhea and/or constipation.

Electricity

Electricity is power. It is the closest indicator of your life force, or energy level. How powerful are you feeling in your life? Is your energy level low, feeling dim, or even dark? Or do you have so much energy and power built up that you 'blow a fuse.' Perhaps you get really worked up over something at work, let it build up, and then one day just blow up at someone. Light bulbs are often the most likely outward manifestation of our energy. You've most likely had one of those days that you flip on a light and the bulb blows. You don't think anything of it until a little later when the same thing happens in another room with another fixture.

Instead of making electrical repairs, sometimes an entire upgrade is necessary. This was the case when I purchased a home that was on the original fuse box system. In older homes, an upgrade to a 200-amp system may be necessary to keep up with today's technology. By upgrading your home's electrical system, you too will get an energy upgrade. You may feel it on the physical or emotional levels or it may be an indication of an increase in spiritual power, awareness, or even vibrational frequency.

The actual **electrical wiring** within the overall electrical system is an indicator of how one channels their energy. Do you live in a home with old, outdated wiring that could run more efficiently if updated? Has your energy been low? Do you have issues with being short-tempered? If not properly wired, energy can be misdirected, causing a short. We run out of steam. Just like our electrical system, how we run our energy can energize or exhaust us.

If our priorities are misaligned, then we become exhausted. The same is true in situations where we give our power away and walk away feeling depleted. On the physical level of the body, this correlates with the nervous system. When our 'wires get crossed,' so to speak, we may feel dizzy, cloudy, or unclear. Other health related issues with the electrical system are blood circulation, chronic fatigue syndrome, and depression.

We control the electricity in our homes via light switches. **Light switches** symbolize the ability to control our power or energy. You can choose to turn the energy on or off. Even better, add dimmers to your switches in order to control your energy with more precision. Dimmer switches allow you to find the perfect balance between the light (yang) and dark (yin), depending on what is necessary in the moment. As such, your energy level will respond accordingly. Dimmer switches are extremely energy efficient since you do not use any more energy than is necessary. The energy is more controlled and lasts much longer similar to that of a marathon runner as opposed to a quick sprinter. The energy of those in the room will receive the same benefits as if the light was completely "on" or "off."

Living "off the grid" has become more and more common as many people no longer want to feel reliant upon the government and municipalities for power. This is a larger movement toward personal power and autonomy as a culture. Those living off the grid are most likely to be independent thinkers with a strong sense of their own power in the world.

Mind Body Home Connection: Electricity

- Do you feel stressed, overworked, or exhausted?
- Are you about to lose your temper?
- Are you mentally cloudy or confused?
- Do you have high blood pressure or other blood circulatory issues?

Internet/Telephone

Living in the Information Age, we've become dependent on the ability to communicate instantly with the internet and smart phones. Facsimiles and land lines are certainly viable means, but no longer as common. Any of these forms of communication are literal symbols for our ability to communicate. When something goes wrong with one of more of these components, the normal channels of communication are literally and figuratively upset.

From an astrological perspective, communication is ruled by planet Mercury. When Mercury is in Retrograde, meaning it appears to be traveling in the opposite direction, communication is often disrupted. During this 2-3 week period, cell phones, fax machines, and other electronic-related items will struggle if there are inherent weaknesses.

Sometimes entire computer systems within a company will go down unexpectedly making communication impossible.

Problems with such devices can also happen if we are having our own personal struggle with communication. For example, I remember a time in which I was avoiding a conversation that I needed to have with a friend. Suddenly my cellphone stopped working properly. It would not allow calls to come through or would simply hang up once I was on the call. After I was finally able to have the conversation I'd been putting off, my phone instantly began working just fine. Our subconscious mind is much more powerful than we give it credit.

The next time you have a malfunction with your phone, Internet, cable, computer, or other communication device consider what the inner message is from your subconscious. Are you avoiding a conversation, reluctant to receiving certain news or information, or procrastinating on a project? Or maybe you just need to be offline to other people for a certain amount of time. Once you become conscious of the message, you'll be amazed at how random glitches may resolve themselves at no cost.

Mind Body Home Connection: Internet/Phone

- Is there a conversation you have been putting off?
- Who or what situation are you avoiding?
- Are you having trouble speaking or being heard?
- Are you experiencing throat-related problems?

Heating and Air Systems

The heating, ventilation, and air conditioning systems, commonly referred to as the HVAC system, represents oxygen, lungs and breathing. The HVAC system of a house relates to the oxygen (air) flow throughout the body, also known as the respiratory system. Just as the breath circulates oxygen throughout our body, the HVAC should ideally circulate air evenly and smoothly throughout the rooms of your home.

Ideally, a space should heat and cool evenly, although this is not always the case due to how rooms are oriented to the Sun or faulty ductwork. Similarly, the body should have proper oxygen flow throughout, although that is not always the case either. Oxygen and blood are the physical manifestation of chi energy. Where chi energy gets cut off or stagnant in the body, there will be a lack of blood and oxygen to that area of the body. This could eventually result in dis-ease of some sort. Oxygen is the body's natural healer. When there is a lack thereof, then there is an imbalance of energy in the body, resulting in dis-ease of some sort. A more common instance of poor circulation is cold hands or feet because the extremities are furthest from the blood pumping heart.

Areas within a home or business that do not get proper air flow is indicative of stagnant energy. This often correlates with the space being of Northern exposure with little sunlight. This in and of itself can make an area more prone to stagnant energy. Homes with a serious disruption of energy as in the case of a ghost or entity will often be located in an area of the home with improper air circulation, either with a lack of air flow or an unusually cold room.

If there are areas within your home that do not circulate properly, then try adding extra lighting, a crystal, a fan, or anything else with energy and movement. Abandoning or ignoring that section of the home is ill-advised as that will further stagnate the energy. You never want to cut off the energy of any part of the home. That is the same as cutting off the energy to a part of your body.

A problem with your HVAC system could correlate with a stressful time in which we have the tendency to clinch and hold our breath as opposed to calming ourselves through breathing. As I mentioned in the Introduction, there was a time in which I owned two houses while moving out of one and into the other. I was stressed to say the least. On the same day at practically the same time, the units in both houses went out. I knew this was not coincidental. I had been so busy that I was exhausted. Both systems happened to need the same part - a fan motor. I was clearly overworking myself and needed to take a breath.

The **air filter** is the component of the HVAC that requires periodic attention in order to keep the air clean by keeping pollutants out. Changing your air filter regularly can guard against this physically and emotionally. By not being conscious of this, we let pollutants into our system without setting up proper filters. What toxins or pollutants are you allowing to infiltrate your space? If you haven't changed your filter lately, think about what else you may not be properly filtering in your life. Not surprisingly, changing filters regularly will make the HVAC system run more efficiently thus saving energy.

Mind Body Home Connection: Heating and Air Systems

- Are you holding your breath or short of breath?
- Do you need to slow down in life?
- Are you overworked?
- Do you have poor circulation or cold extremities?

CHAPTER 12

OUTDOOR SPACES: HOW WE RELATE TO OTHERS

Don't ever take a fence down until you know why it was put up.

—Robert Frost

- Front and Back of Home
- Front Porch
- Patio/Deck
- Balcony
- Fence
- Garden
- Driveway
- Swimming Pool
- Trees

By now, you are probably seeing your home in a whole new light with an understanding of how it is a representation of yourself - physically, mentally, and emotionally. And as you make changes to your home, you make changes to yourself. As we begin to move out of the actual house and into the outdoor spaces, you will start seeing how you relate to others in the world beyond those with whom you are cohabitating.

Our outdoor spaces, such as the yard, deck, patio, or balcony, are aspects of ourselves. Just as these spaces extend beyond the physical house, they energetically connect us with the rest of the world. When we step outside into our outdoor spaces, we do so to commune with others - whether it is nature, neighbors, or our perceived public.

There are varying degrees of outdoor spaces depending on the type of living space. For example, most single-family homes have a yard, while a condo space may have a balcony at most. Some living spaces may even have shared outdoor spaces, such as a rooftop garden area in a high-rise condo unit. In this instance, the outdoor space is communal in nature, which is commensurate with the social lifestyle of condo living. Those who live in a home with no outdoor space at all may experience a stark contrast between private and public spaces. This is usually the case in large metropolitan areas where space is at a premium and social living takes precedence. With no transition from one to the other, they may find themselves seeking an equivalent area at a nearby park or coffee shop.

On the other extreme, some seek solitude and desire more space between their private life and the rest of the world. Accordingly, country or farm life is more appealing to some. The more yard or acreage, the more distance you desire from the rest of the world. Whether a simple balcony or acres of farmland, the space that extends beyond our homestead represent our arm's length or bridge between our private life and public persona. Let's take a look at each of these aspects in more detail.

Front and Back of Home

A friend once shared a dream with me. In the dream, her front yard looked like a normal, sunny, neighborhood yard, while in the backyard it was pouring raining as she stood at the edge of a cliff. At the time, she was giving the appearance that all was well in her life, while in reality she was at a major crossroads paralyzed in fear. Her dream is an example of the stark symbolic differences between the front and back yard. The **front yard** is our public persona, or what we want the public to see. The **back yard**, on the other hand, is what we don't want the rest of the world to see. It represents aspects of ourselves that we would rather just keep private from the world. They are in essence a flip side of the same coin.

You might wonder how this differs from the symbolism of closet and storage spaces. We are aware of what is going on in our backyard - we just don't want others to know. Whereas, with regard to a closet, we are not even aware of what lurks inside because it is buried too deep within our subconscious to face it. The backyard is more exposed than our storage spaces in that it is viewable by us, our close friends, and neighbors, but not to the world at large.

The backyard represents hidden aspects, or our shadow side, of ourselves in how we relate to the world. While you may give the appearance to your friends and coworkers that everything is great, i.e. nice front yard, you may actually be unhappy and confused about your life, i.e. unkept back yard, as represented in my friend's dream. Or perhaps the opposite is true. Sometimes our backyard is where our true sanctuary lies hidden from the world. This is often the case with shy or quiet people.

In the case of one client, her front yard was in dire need of yard maintenance with weeds and fallen leaves overtaking the yard. But I was astonished when I went to her backyard. It was a beautiful oasis of flowers and artfully placed yard décor. While most of the backyard was well-loved, it was the Love corner of the yard (based upon the Bagua Map) where the heart of the beauty lay. She admitted that she experienced a real disconnect between her reputation at work as being bossy and rigid with her relationship at home as being soft and loving. This was a great example of hiding or not expressing our true beauty into the world.

In order to live a truly authentic life, it is best to connect these two worlds into one. I advised my client to add a pathway from the front yard into the back yard in order to connect her two worlds. We often hide the best parts of ourselves from the world. Other times, we put up a false front in how we show up in the world. By bringing the "back yard" forward and the "front yard" back, we start to combine these aspects to bring forth a whole, authentic expression of ourselves into the world. If the front and back yards are separated by a fence, then it is important to have a door or gate opening that allows access to and from the front and back yards. Like all doors within a home, the door or gate should be operational and easily opened and closed so that there is no discord between the energy of the front yard and back yard.

Think about whether you spend more time in your front yard or back yard. This could include leisure time enjoying the outdoor spaces or work time tending to the lawn or gardens. Where is your favorite outdoor spot? For myself, when I'm feeling more social, I will take a book or my computer and spend time on my front porch. At those times, I enjoy seeing people walk by and waving to neighbors. At other times when I am feeling more introverted, I will head to the back deck.

Do you spend more time working on the front yard or back yard? In which space have you planted more gardens or maintained the lawn with more effort? Notice where you are intuitively drawn the next time you are inspired to work in the yard. At times, you may have a desire to work on your outward appearance, such as buying a new outfit, while other times, you may be drawn to work on your inner self, such as a massage or therapy service. The same is true with your yard spaces. At times, you may be drawn to the front yard and other times the back yard.

Also consider the condition of the yard when you buy a house. It may be indicative of what you need to work on in order to balance your public and private sides. Think back to your past homes. What was the condition of the yards before and after you lived there? Did you make improvements or simply maintain the existing yard? Think about how this may have correlated with what you were experiencing at that time in your life with regard to your public life.

In one particular home I lived in, the backyard was in complete disarray upon purchasing it, while the front yard and landscaping looked beautiful. The backyard had little grass and a lot of construction trash, weeds, and overgrown areas. With attention and hard work over two years, the backyard was transformed and looked fabulous with a vegetable garden, hammock, and zen garden. A new sidewalk was put in joining the front and backyard with a beautiful doorway connecting the two. With this upgrade, I experienced a sense of integration in bringing my authentic self into the world.

Front Porch

There is nothing more inviting than a large front porch furnished with rocking chairs and a swing. It is a style quintessential to bungalows and craftsmen homes. Unfortunately, the front porch has become a lost architectural feature, although the style is being replicated in many planned neighborhoods. A front porch represents your social self or façade. It's how you portray yourself to others. If you have a front porch, think about what it says about you. What kind of seating is there? A single chair for reading? Or are you more social and welcoming of friends and neighbors stopping by with comfy seating and a coffee table setting? Or is your front porch empty with little of your personality showing through? Consider how you want to be perceived socially and make changes to your front porch accordingly if there is a mismatch.

Occasionally, the front porch is in need of disrepair. In the case of a concrete front porch, it could experience cracks or crackling paint. Wood front porches are occasionally in need of repair to the floorboards. In these cases, consider if there has been a sense of social withdrawal. Have you been fending off social interactions and engagements for some reason? If so, consider why and if it is still serving you in some way. Upon repairing the porch, you will experience a return to normal social involvement.

***Mind Body Home Connection:* Front Porch**
- Are you happy with your level of social interactions?
- Do you desire more social time?
- Are there people you are avoiding?
- What face are you putting forward?
- Are you being seen or portrayed in an accurate light?

Patio/Deck

A patio or deck extends the house into the back yard creating more outdoor living space. In creating more physical space, it also creates more mental space for the occupants. Have you ever seen the back of a home with no patio or deck? The house just stops abruptly. There is no transition and the energy stops abruptly as if something is missing. A patio or deck extends the energy of the home giving its occupants more space in which to open up into, express themselves, and explore new aspects of themselves.

In feng shui, patios and decks are considered extensions of the Bagua Map and thus provide bonus areas in which to expand. For example, if you have a patio off the back right of your home, it would be considered an extension of your Love Corner and off the back left of your home would be an extension of your Wealth Corner. Whereas, a deck or patio centered off the back of the home would give the Fame & Reputation section a boost for the occupants. Of course, it could also be an energy drain if not properly maintained or used.

If you have a deck or patio extending from your home, notice where it is in relation to the Bagua Map. It could also take up multiple sections, if not the entire back of the home. Take advantage of this extra energy by using these outdoor spaces. Avoid letting these areas go ignored or in need of repair. Otherwise, it will deplete the energy from the correlating sections of the Bagua Map. Keep plants healthy. Add outdoor lighting or other accents to give the area a boost of energy.

Mind Body Home Connection: **Patio/Deck**
- Are you taking advantage of available opportunities?
- Are you ignoring opportunities or squandering them away?
- Do you need a boost of energy or another outlet to utilize your energy?
- What talent or skill are you underutilizing?

Balcony

A balcony is often associated with romance, chivalry, and royalty. It is the damsel in distress pleading from the balcony to be saved or Romeo beckoning Juliet to come down from the balcony. In matters of pomp and circumstance, politicians and even the Pope speak from a balcony. Inherent to a balcony is that it is high above the ground automatically putting the person on the balcony in a higher position than those on the ground. In terms of our living spaces, a balcony represents what is special about us - our traits, talents, and skills that set us apart from others.

If you have a balcony, be sure to take advantage of this space and make it yours. Do not let the space go unused or ignored as this represents a skill or talent that you are not utilizing. You will often see this with homes with multiple outdoor spaces that include a balcony, perhaps off a bedroom. While the homeowners may have had plans for it or even loved it initially, it ends up never getting used. Whereas in loft or condo spaces, the balcony may be the only outdoor space available in which case it is used frequently. Either way, be aware of this space and maximize its potential.

Mind Body Home Connection: **Balcony**
- Are you utilizing your special skills and talents?
- What aspects of yourself are you underutilizing?
- Do you need to lift yourself up or boost your confidence?
- Are you waiting for someone to show up and save you?

Fence

Fences are common in urban areas where homes are situated in close proximity to one another. A fence is a boundary that literally and figuratively draws a line in the sand. Likewise, a fence represents setting a boundary in our own life. Creating healthy boundaries can be challenging for many people. It is usually in the context of family and friends, although sometimes so is the case with nosy neighbors. A fence is a literal boundary between you and your immediate neighbor or property line, but it can also represent boundaries on a larger scale as well.

Have you ever had to replace part of a fence? Maybe a fence collapsed due to degradation or a fallen tree. Or maybe you installed a fence in the ground for the first time. If you have experienced any of these, then most likely you were also setting, creating, or clarifying boundaries in some relationship in your life during that time. Repairing a fence can help mend relationships by resetting appropriate boundaries.

Are you feeling "on the fence" about a particular situation in your life? This could be an alternative meaning in the event of a fence suddenly falling on your property. When we are on the fence about something in our life, we feel stuck and unable to commit to one thing or the other. Sometimes we need to be nudged in one direction or the other. This could manifest into an unexpected collapse of a fence from a storm, tree, or other unordinary, or even unexplainable, event.

Mind Body Home Connection: Fence

- Where do you need to set boundaries in your life?
- Is there a particular relationship that has crossed a boundary?
- Are you feeling "on the fence" about a certain situation?
- Do you need to draw a line in the sand with someone?
- Do you need to make an important decision?

Garden

Garden spaces come in many forms - from vegetable gardens to flower gardens to simple shrubs. Regardless of their shape, size and contents, they symbolize abundance and prosperity. Homes with luscious landscapes give the appearance of abundance despite the size or location of the home. The same is true for cities that are blessed with weather conducive to growing flowers and fruit year-round. There is an abundance about the city and usually commensurate with the cost of living as well.

Even homes without a yard can have beautiful container gardens on a porch or balcony in order to connect with nature and its abundant properties. While there is an entire subcategory within feng shui pertaining to gardens, the *number one* rule is to grow plants and flowers that are native to your region. Of course, the most important aspect to any garden is that it be healthy and alive. An abundant garden takes just the right balance of sun, water, and minerals, which follows the Five Elements cycle in feng shui.

Just as important as having healthy plants is keeping your garden weeded. There are many clichés about weeding your garden with regard to keeping relationships maintained and healthy. This has become part of our collective consciousness to the point of literally manifesting. The next time you weed your garden consider what part of your life needs weeding as well. Is it a particular relationship or is it an aspect of yourself that you have been neglecting? Once you have weeded the garden, consider whether it's time to plant something new or whether the empty space feels better.

Mind Body Home Connection: Gardens

- Are you feeling abundant and prosperous?
- Are you taking care of yourself and tending to your own garden?
- What weeds do you need to pull in your life?
- Do you need to nurture yourself to facilitate your own growth?
- Are you feeling "dead" or stagnant?

Driveway

The driveway of a house is made specifically for the car and therefore symbolically relates more to our car than our home. That being said, the driveway is that connection point or transitional space between our home and the rest of the world via our car. Our car symbolizes how we go through life. Most everyone at some time has had a dream of driving a car. Maybe in your dream the road was icy. Maybe you were swerving or driving out of control. Or maybe your car was stolen. These dreams indicate how in control of our life we are feeling at the time. Our car can also represent our ambition in life and perhaps even our status in the world depending on how much we value our car.

The driveway is an inherent pathway and thus represents our own path as we leave the safety of our home and go into the unpredictability and unknown world. Through our driveway we leave our comfort zone. It is a transition space between the known and the unknown. The larger the property, the longer the driveway will most likely be thereby creating a larger buffer for transitioning. If you live in an urban area, then you may not have a driveway at all. The transition may be the sidewalk that leads you to the street where your car is parked. This sudden transition may be too jarring for some people.

Driveways are usually permanent fixtures and often go ignored. Depending on the surface, they usually need periodic sealing to avoid cracking. In the case of a rock driveway, new rock may need to be added as it weathers. Otherwise, little maintenance is required. Upgrading or improving a driveway however can give the homeowners a smoother path in life. Also consider what activities take place in the driveway. It is a place where random accidents sometimes happen, such as running over a personal belonging. Obstacles in the driveway represent obstacles in your life. Consider whether such an obstacle occurs when leaving your home or when coming home. The timing will indicate whether it represents an obstacle within your household or in the workplace.

***Mind Body Home Connection*: Driveway**
- Are you having difficulty knowing your path in life?
- Do you feel like you are driving on smooth pavement or a gravel road?
- What is getting in the way of your ambitions and goals?
- Do you feel like obstacles are getting in your way?
- What keeps getting in your way?

Swimming Pool

Swimming pools are an outdoor element that can either add or detract from the energy of the home. Not coincidentally, a pool can also dramatically increase or decrease the value of a home depending on the circumstances. By their very nature, swimming pools are containers of water used for the purpose of recreation and relaxing. When used and taken care of, a swimming pool is a beneficial energy that adds to the household in a way that is hard to replicate.

If the pool is not taken care of, unused, or neglected, then it can be an energy drain, literally and figuratively. If you have a swimming pool in such a condition, then consider in what area of your life you are feeling drained. Where are you underutilizing your energy? Is there anything more depressing than seeing a swimming pool without water? A large empty vat in your backyard is not only a safety hazard, but an emotional and financial wasteland. This scenario should be avoided at all costs.

In feng shui, a swimming pool is a strong Water element. If a home is located on property with water, such as a lake or ocean, then consideration should be given as to whether a pool will add too much of the water element. Too much water can lead to an overload of emotions and feeling ungrounded. A feng shui professional can help you with this assessment depending on the other elements surrounding the property. For example, if the home is located in an already moist environment, then adding more water is not advisable. However, if the location is in a sunny location, then the water will help balance out the fire element from the Sun.

The location of the pool with regard to the Bagua Map is another important consideration. For example, if the pool is located in the back center of the home, in the Fame & Reputation section, then the water element would need to be balanced by adding more fire elements using décor and finishes. This can involve a complex balance of the Five Element Theory used in feng shui due to the pool being a strong Water element. For more information on balancing the elements, I recommend my book, *Decorating With the Five Elements of Feng Shui*.

Mind Body Home Connection: Swimming Pool

- Do you feel overly emotional or ungrounded?
- Do you feel like your energy is being drained?
- Do you feel emotionally drained?

Trees

For many people, their favorite memories growing up revolved around a tree in their yard. Trees can add an important energetic component providing a safe, protective place for introspection, a place for shade, and in the case of Buddha, a place for awakening. Trees are an important metaphor for our own energy as they strike the perfect balance between being grounded and expanding at the same time. Simply having one strong and sturdy tree in your yard can help ground the home and its occupants.

But what happens when a tree falls on your property? If the tree or limb fell as a result of a storm, then there is a clearing energy. Storms balance the energy in the atmosphere. They clear away stagnant energy that has collected. And in doing so, storms can be destructive often clearing away trees and limbs. In this case, the trees or limbs are representative of something that needs to be cleared from our own life. Similar to clutter, fallen trees and limbs represent what no longer serves our highest and best interest. It is making space for more light to come through.

Storm winds can sometimes completely uproot a tree. Storm winds represent "winds of change." An uprooted tree is the physical representation of this change. In fact, the change is so extreme that it has the energy of uprooting us. This could uproot an old belief system that is no longer serving you. It could represent something groundbreaking that has come into your life or something that has shaken your own foundation, perhaps during a stressful or transitional time in life.

Sometimes a tree will fall for no apparent reason. This happened to me a few years ago. Within a few days of moving into my house, I came home one night to find a tree taking up the entire driveway. It had fallen in the exact spot my car had been parked. The strangest part was that it was a calm, still summer night with absolutely no wind. There was no explanation as to why the tree had fallen, let alone been uprooted. Energetically, however, the move into this house marked a considerable shift in my life that clearly had shaken me to the core.

Mind Body Home Connection: Trees

- What needs to be cleared from your life?
- What is no longer serving you?
- Are your support systems falling away?
- What foundation systems have shifted?
- What belief systems are no longer supporting you?
- What has shaken your foundation?

CHAPTER 13

ENCROACHMENTS: WHAT WE ATTRACT

[E]verything in the unconscious seeks outward manifestation.

—Carl Jung

- Ants
- Flies
- Cockroaches
- Mice
- Burglar
- Ghosts

As our energy and the energy of our home come together, our home sends us messages in and around the home that reveal our subconscious desires, fears, and thoughts. As you have seen from the previous chapters, everything seeks outward manifestation in some form or another. In the same vein, we also attract certain things into our home as well. These usually come in the form of insects, rodents, or other entities that take up our energy. Where we have energetic holes in our life and thus in our home, it allows space for other energy to take up and use. As such, we attract others to come in and take up our space. Similar to an old friend crashing on your couch, we unconsciously invite other energies into our space.

You've most likely experienced an infestation of a certain type of insect in your home at some point. And while certain insects are prone to certain regions at certain times of the year, it is nevertheless not coincidental. For example, where I live spiders are common in the Fall. Regardless however, I have lived in some homes where spiders were never an issue and other homes less than a mile away where spiders were a major problem. As such, certain homes attract certain insects depending on the moisture and lighting. And thus in some cases the energy of the home is a stronger factor in what outside energies are attracted inside.

Nothing seems to bring out fear in people more than bugs, insects, or rodents. Most everyone has a strong aversion to some sort of bug, spider, or small animal. We all have our *Achilles Heel* as to what gives us the heebee-jeebees. Usually it goes back to childhood and to what we were exposed. Other times, it may be completely unexplainable. I grew up in a house in the woods where spiders were very common and, to this day I have no problem with spiders. However, the thought of a mouse, let alone seeing one, will send me to the roof. These little creatures represent an aspect of ourselves that is unrealized, similar to our shadow side. For example, there are attributes of a mouse that I need to own. Thus these creatures show up in our spaces as a reminder, or a resonance.

In considering the following encroachments, think back to whether you have ever experienced these and what was going on at that time in your life. For future referencing, if you begin experiencing any of these energies in your home, consider what the message is for you. Why has this energy shown up in your space? Remember how it entered and in what room. Once conscious of it, you may be surprised as to how quickly the energy leaves. An exterminator may still be in order however for good measure.

Ants

Is there anything more annoying than having ants in your home? Have you ever had an ant infestation show up out of nowhere? Not surprisingly, ants represent annoyances. When they suddenly show up in your home, they are a manifestation of some annoyance or irritation in your daily life. Ants also represent petty annoyances that seem insignificant, but they can also build up similar to an anthill. Before long, it becomes something much bigger that represents a general dissatisfaction in your daily life.

It's no coincidence that while ants are highly annoying, they're also extremely efficient and one of the most organizational-minded energies on the planet. Annoyances and pettiness can also cause one to be inefficient in how one uses their energy and goes about their day. They represent industry, productivity, and efficiency. Consider where in your life you can use more organization and efficiency. Annoyances are distractions. And distractions take our focus and energy into nonproductive outlets. Where are you being distracted? Also consider in what room or area of your home the ants appear. The location of the annoyances may give more information about the message.

Flies

"What's bugging you?" Flying insects are synonymous with swatting, clapping, and waving them to remove them from our personal space. Like ants, flies are annoying irritants as well, although there is an air quality about them that makes them more elusive than ants. They cause us to become ungrounded as we swat them away, becoming mentally distracted in the process. While ants represent annoyances in our physical world, flies represent mental annoyances that come and go through our mind.

Ants show us the gift of productivity, while flies have a unique gift of transformation. Flies transform sludge. It is the reason they seek decay, waste, and anything dead. They are transforming this energy. If you come across an inordinate number of flies in your home, then consider what is dead, dying, or decaying in your life that needs transforming. What mental thoughts are no longer serving you and only distracting you?

Cockroaches

Just writing about cockroaches is difficult, let alone seeing one. While cockroaches are nasty little insects that we associate with foraging for food and crawling in unwelcomed places, they actually deliver a powerful message. Cockroaches are similar to weeds in that if the world were to end, they would be the lone survivors. Cockroaches have incredible survival skills. They scurry, squeeze, and elude danger at all costs.

My only serious encounter with cockroaches was my first apartment in law school. It is not coincidental that I was in survival mode in my first year in moving to a new city not knowing anyone. By the time I moved out of this apartment, I had integrated into my new life and established friendships, never experience cockroaches again, nor the feeling of survival. Seeing cockroaches can also signify one's own need for rejuvenation or self-cleaning on the emotional or spiritual levels, or needing to eradicate negative thoughts.

Mice

Mice represent holes in our life, also indicative of energy leaks. I had one particular situation that gave me new insight about mice. I had just moved into a newly renovated, historic home. Prior to the renovation an older man lived in the house for decades. This was, not coincidentally, the same home I mentioned earlier that came with a ghost. The first cold, October evening around dusk, I realized we were not alone, but shared the space with mice as I saw one run across the kitchen floor. I screamed. Traps and bait were set, but there was a sense that there were multiple mice. My dog was sniffing in odd places and that's never a good sign. After several days of feeling uneasy, I got to the point that I didn't want to be home after dusk. I was literally being run out of my own home by mice!

I realized this was crazy and I began to wonder what the meaning of all this was. It hit me that I was not taking up my own space. In other words, I was not using my power. I was underutilizing myself and allowing others to overpower me. If you don't take up your space, then someone or something else will – whether it's a mouse, a competitor, your mother, or even a friend.

The old man who had lived there for years apparently had not minded his furry friends and thus the mice were allowed to run rampant. I was an intruder upon their space. When I realized that this was what was happening in my own home – that I energetically had not claimed the space as mine yet – I got to work. I was tired of being fearful of mice. I was tired of something else taking over my home. I felt a new sense of power that I had never felt before. I declared it as my home and completely filled every corner and nook & cranny with my energy through meditation. This was my house. I started to consider where else in my life I had not been taking up my rightful space.

Often people have problems with mice upon moving into a new house. Perhaps the house had been sitting empty for a while or the previous owners weren't as tidy. In either case, you are being asked to claim your space and your power. Mice inevitably enter the home through holes. The holes have as much symbolism as the mice. Holes, even if the size of a dime, indicate holes in your life. Where are you letting energy escape? Where in your life or in your relationships are there holes? What is not being discussed in your household?

The gift that a mouse offers is that of resourcefulness, adaptability, timidness over arrogance, and tidiness. If you find a mouse in your living space, then consider if any of these attributes are qualities of which you need to embody more.

Burglar

Anything that comes into our space that has not been invited is an intrusion of our energy and our space. Like insects and rodents, burglars are an example of allowing others to take our space. It may be hard to imagine that victims of burglary have on some level attracted the energy of allowing an invasion. And while random accidents and incidents happen without explanation, usually there is a resonance that allowed the intrusive energy. Anyone who has had their home broken into will tell you that it feels like a personal assault, or even a violation of their physical body. This of course speaks to the strong energetic connection between the home and the body. When our home has been intruded, our personal energy has as well.

There are several messages pertaining to a burglary of your home. Because it is more akin to a physical invasion, then the message will most definitely hit home on a much deeper and personal level. It may take some time to recover and fully understand the meaning and message because of the trauma surrounding it. The energy around a burglary is that of violation as it inevitably involves a "breaking in." Is there an area in your life in which you are feeling violated, whether it is a particular relationship, job or situation?

Another meaning is that an unconscious aspect of yourself is attempting to make itself conscious. If you've ever seen the remnants of a home invasion, you know that every drawer, shelf, and cabinet may be completely unearthed and scattered in plain sight. Ready or not, you are forced to 'clean up' things that you perhaps have not dealt with in years. This was the case with my client. Her break-in brought to light just how much clutter she had accumulated. She acknowledged that the break-in was a "wake-up call" for where she was in her life. In cleaning up the remnants, she realized how much she needed to clean out of her life in order to allow new things to come in.

If you've had your home broken into, it's paramount that you space clear your home. The home itself experiences trauma and must heal appropriately. In space clearing clients' homes, several times I've come across a specific area with an energy disturbance. When I ask my client about the area, it was in fact the entry area in which someone broke into the home years before. Secondly, it's important to remove the energy of the intruder and clear the resulting trauma from the homeowners.

Ghosts

Ghosts are another intrusive energy that we attract. Whether you move into a home with a ghost or attract one later, there is an energetic tie or resonance between the ghost and the occupants. Ghosts, in general, relate to past energy that continues to linger. So is the case with a ghost in your home - it relates to unfinished emotional business from your past. This could include unresolved emotions or issues relating to your childhood family, dead relatives, or repressed memories and feelings. In essence, the ghost carries an energy that you are seeking and vice versa. Refer to Chapter 5 for more information on ghosts.

CONCLUSION

INTEGRATING YOUR MIND BODY AND HOME

Our contribution to the progress of the world must consist in setting our own house in order.

—Mahatma Ghandi

You are most likely seeing your home in a whole new light. The power our living spaces have in our lives has been vastly underestimated. Our home is so close to us that we often have a hard time seeing the forest for the trees. When we stop and look around our space with new eyes, there is a world of opportunity to heal, empower, and to step into a higher consciousness. It is literally right under our nose. Our space holds the power of transformation. As we make changes to our home, we make changes to ourself.

Chances are you've worked on some aspect of self-improvement - therapy, energy work, meditation, or yoga. Like most things, the change has to take place on the inner in order to make permanent changes in our outer life. It is often hard to measure when we make beneficial changes in our life until they manifest outwardly in our life. But our home is a physical manifestation of our thoughts and emotions. We can see the changes with our own eyes. And we can also see what needs to change by noticing the messages it communicates to us.

When we see our living space in disarray, we know that our life is in disarray. When we see our home undergoing a renovation, we know that some aspect of our life is under renovation. When suddenly we can't get into our own home because the lock is sticking, then we know there is a troubling issue that we are not facing. Our home manifests into the physical world our thoughts and emotions that we would otherwise dismiss and put aside. However, in becoming conscious of our unconscious, we enter a higher consciousness that is necessary for our spiritual growth.

As you start to become more conscious of your living space, consider the variety of ways in which your home is communicating with you, as well as how you can make conscious changes in your life. Changes are manifested through household accidents, improvements, general maintenance, repairs, renovations, and even in moving. Each of these holds a different meaning or energy, particularly when we are proactive and initiate a change versus when something goes wrong or accidental. As each of these come up in your life consider the meaning and message and how it mirrors what is going on within yourself.

Household Accidents

In Chapter 6 we looked at how electronics are good indicators of how our energy affects objects because they either work properly or malfunction. The same is true for all inanimate objects. Just because they are not operational, all objects are symbols with a meaning of some sort in our life, or else we wouldn't possess them. Instead of malfunctioning, we might accidentally knock a vase off the shelf or repeatedly break an item. For example, a few years ago I was going through a stressful time. Within a few weeks, I broke two toothbrush handles while brushing my teeth and then a teapot handle. Both of these breaks are extremely difficult to do not to mention, quite odd. I finally got the message that I was having trouble getting a 'handle' on things. Once I became conscious of the message, I realized I needed to "get a grip" and relax. Handles stopped breaking thereafter.

Accidents may occur even more randomly. Have you ever had an object fall in the middle of the night with no explanation? This has happened to me many times in different homes - a bathroom mirror, a ceiling light, a window decoration. Besides waking me in complete terror, there was a message with each incident. In the same way we manifest nightmares to get our attention, sometimes it takes a frightening event in our home to get our attention.

The next time you have something that breaks, falls, or malfunctions, consider whether there is an underlying message. Is it more than a random incident, or is there a deeper meaning? Where did the object come from? Did someone give it to you? Who or what does it remind you of? What are you thinking about at the time the accident occurred? Also consider the symbolism of the object that is involved in the incident. Consult a dream dictionary for its symbolism on the collective conscious. That being said, objects can also hold the energy that we give them. A picture of your family on your desk holds the energy that you have toward your family. Thus, that picture has a significant energy and symbolism specific to you.

Personal accidents around the home happen far too commonly, ranging from stubbing your toe to falling down the stairs. When these unfortunate accidents occur, they too may have a message. Beyond the mind body relationship, the location within your home is significant information. For example, did you trip going up or down the stairs? Did you stub your toe in the bedroom or in the kitchen? Consider the location of each accident and consult the corresponding chapter in this book for more insight.

Repairs and Maintenance

Have you ever felt like you can never get around to making improvements to your home because you're too busy fixing things? Or maybe you spend so much energy on just maintaining your home that there is neither time nor money left for improvements. There was a time in my life when maintaining the yard took so much time that I never had time to plant new flowerbeds. Or maybe you would love to splurge on some new bed linens, but know you need to get the gutters fixed. It is only when you get your head above water that you are able to make improvements. And so is the case in our own life. For example, you know you need to start cooking healthy meals, but can't seem to find the time or energy after work to do so. Or you would love to get in shape with an exercise regimen, but get set back with an illness or injury.

If you feel like there are improvement projects around your home that you would like to do, but just can't seem to get around to them, then take a look to see if this is also happening in your own life. Sometimes we feel we are just trying to make it through the day, let alone take steps to *improve* our life. If this sounds familiar to you, take a conscious look at what you have trouble maintaining. Once you learn the message, you can then move on from it and begin making the desired improvements.

Do you have something that keeps breaking or in constant need of repair? Or is keeping your house clean overwhelmingly difficult? If it is a pattern, recognize it. What is your house trying to tell you? Oftentimes, recognizing the problem is all that is necessary to stop the cycle. In more severe cases, you may desire to seek from a professional. Many times, taking action to remedy the issue in the home will happen simultaneously with addressing the issue within yourself.

For example, one time I was seeing a craniosacral therapist following a concussion I experienced. Upon arriving home following my appointment, the special-ordered light bulbs for the home's outdoor lighting had arrived. They had been burned out since moving in. I installed the new lights, and viola, my concussion symptoms eased. Was it from the craniosacral appointment, or the lightbulb moment? Both simultaneously.

Many of my clients are overwhelmed with where to start in their home. In some cases, my job as a feng shui consultant is more of a project manager by helping prioritize the order of projects rather than anything else. As a general rule, repairs take first priority. Having broken, inoperable, or damaged parts of a home is equivalent to an illness or injury within the body. The energy emanates from the injury and lowers the overall vibration.

Just like the body, when there is an injury, the blood flows to that section to try to heal the area. As a result, the rest of the body is affected in order to keep some semblance of balance within the system. The same is the case with our home. If you have an area with water damage, this is like an injury to the home that lowers the overall vibration of the home. If not repaired, the damage will start to creep and infect other parts of the home.

It is advisable to not keep even small items or appliances around that are broken, for example, a toaster, lamp, or even a cracked frame. Our subconscious mind picks up the energy of something being broken. Even if you're not thinking about it consciously, the subconscious mind registers the energy of "broken," "cracked," "tarnished," or whatever state the object is in each time you enter that room. I had one client who kept a bird figurine on her kitchen windowsill. One of the wings had broken off, but she couldn't bear to get rid of it. When I asked her why, she said the bird reminds her of herself. I encouraged her to let the item go when she was ready to fly. When she became aware of the symbolism and how it was keeping her from her dreams and desires, she let the item go and never looked back.

Improvements

When you make repairs to your home, you are inherently improving yourself as well. The overall energy of the home returns to balance and restores order within the home. When you voluntarily make an improvement to your home, you are consciously making a self-improvement of yourself as well. When you are conscious of the effects of your improvement, the change can take place in an even more profound way.

For example, once I had finally completed an overall updating of the plumbing, electricals, and HVAC to just *maintain* normal living conditions in my home, I was ready to start an *improvement* project. This time it would be because I wanted to improve my home, not because it was vitally necessary. I knew I had reached a new level of growth within myself at this point. I decided to paint the exterior trim of the taupe, adobe-style house to add some curb appeal.

I set out to paint the brickwork around the windows a red brick color and the window trim turquoise to bring out its charm and character. With each window its personality became more and more apparent. It then hit me one day while painting that the exact thing was happening in my own life. After spending a year 'fixing' things in my life and starting to feel whole again, my personality was now coming out. I was coming out of my shell, so to speak. The quiet, shy, blend-in taupe house transformed into its own unique expression catching the eye of all who drove by.

You may be wondering if you must do the labor yourself to have the correlating effect. Just having the intention and following through with it is enough, whether you hire the labor out or do it yourself. The energy of transformation is in the home and as the home undergoes the change, so will your energy on some level. That being said, if you decide to take on the project yourself, you may gain even more awareness. A friend of mine decided to tile her kitchen herself without having any prior tiling experience. During the project, she experienced much angst, frustration, and crying, all the time grieving a past relationship. All of the frustration she experienced with tiling was the perfect catalyst she needed to release old emotions.

Upon finishing the project, she had completely transformed her kitchen and herself. As she was ripping up the five layers of old linoleum to find a rotted-out hole in the subflooring, she realized you can't hide the past by putting more layers over it. To truly start fresh, you have to go to the root of the problem and fix it there before you can really move on. Of course, it is not coincidental that it was the kitchen, as it is symbolic of the heart of the home, nurturing, and spiritual transformation. The brand-new floor also gave her a greater sense of feeling grounded in herself than she had ever before experienced. Interestingly, she met her partner a few weeks later.

As you set out to make improvements notice in which area of the home you're making the improvement. Or is it a particular component, such as a new roof, plumbing, or couch? Maybe you are decorating a room. What room is it and what is the correlating meaning of the room? Also notice where the room or area falls on the Bagua Map. Is your Wealth Corner getting a boost? Consider the meanings of each and what resonates with you the most.

Renovation

A renovation project is a major improvement to your home and will mirror a renovation of yourself in some aspect. A renovation of a home significantly shifts the energy as it usually involves adding, subtracting, or moving walls and perhaps even mechanicals and fixtures. It is important to bless or space clear the home after a renovation project to help ground the energy. Are you renovating the entire home or just a room or section? Again, consider what room or area of the house and where it falls on the Bagua Map for more clarity on what aspect is being renovated within yourself.

Prior to a renovation project, consider consulting with a feng shui professional. All too often a renovation, particularly in the form of an add-on, will shift the energy negatively. Renovating a home may involve interior, cosmetic touches, such as stripping wallpaper and changing light fixtures. But it also may involve completely changing the shape or floor plan of the house by taking down or extending out walls. It is important to understand the implications when adding on to homes.

In adding an addition, this often creates a Missing Corner in the floor plan thereby creating an imbalance of energy. Another common problem is confusing the energy in the home. When the original blueprints are created for a home and subsequently built, the energy is embedded into the home. When rooms are shifted around for different purposes, the energy conflicts with the original energy of the home. It will take some time for the new energy to ground into the space. If the changes are too incongruent with the "soul of the home," then this could result in a more permanent imbalance.

For example, in my current home I was looking forward to building a screened-in porch on the back. To do so, a window on the exterior wall would need to be replaced with a door that would lead into the screened-in porch. It made sense structurally and aesthetically. However, every time it came time to move forward with the plans, an uneasy feeling would creep up. It related to the back wall, which was a beautiful exposed brick wall with a picturesque window. It felt like the backbone of the house and I got an intuitive message that it was not to be messed with as it would significantly disturb the energy of the house. I felt relief from the home when we decided not to go forward with the plans.

In making major changes to your home, intuitively check in with your home as to whether the change will energetically benefit the soul of the home. If not, then the renovation will not benefit the household either. The change also needs to be in harmony with the original style and intent of the house. All too often you will see an obvious add-on to a house that is of a lower quality or completely different materials than the original house. Also keep in mind that anytime major work is done on your home, particularly in removing or adding walls, this is equivalent to a surgery on your home. It will take some time for the space to heal and integrate the new energy. A space clearing is advised to assist this process.

That is not to say that homes cannot be significantly renovated or added on. Clearly, some homes have ineffective floor plans that need to be rebuilt. Adding on to homes can also provide its occupants with the energy of adding on some new skill, talent, or untapped aspect of themselves. This can also be effective for couples needing a fresh start in their relationship.

Tearing down old homes that are beyond repair is common in areas of gentrification. If it costs more to rebuild the home than build a new one from scratch, the builder will opt for the latter. When a home is torn down, the original energetic blueprint remains in place. This can possibly cause an energetic disturbance with the new home. Because the energy is still in place with the previous home, it can be challenging for the energy of the new home to ground in on the same lot. It is advisable to have a feng shui professional or space clearer to clear the land and the remnants of the previous energy. The homeowners may opt for conducting their own ceremony or blessing of the land.

This type of energy disturbance may become more of an issue when it comes time to sell the home. This is often when energy disturbances from the land will rear their heads. In a way, the home is asking to be healed and brought into balance. When we can't sell a home, we often become more proactive and desperate in our measures. Although usually unconscious of this, we seek to bring balance to the home by making repairs, planting flowers, decorating, and perhaps even hiring a feng shui professional. Although we are doing it to sell the home, we're also healing the home which allows us to move on.

Renting Your Home

As a result of the housing crash in 2008, many homeowners found themselves as landlords. Without the ability to sell their home, but with the need to move for a job or relationship, many people ended up renting their home. I found myself in this predicament. I thought being a landlord would be easy. I found great tenants who paid like clockwork and appreciated the home.

However, within a few months, I started getting phone calls about random issues - from leaks to freak accidents to pest issues. None of these were issues I had ever experienced while living there. What I realized was that their energy was manifesting through the home in random accidents and urgent maintenance needs. The home was in constant need of repairs beyond anything I had experienced while living there.

It is common knowledge that renters will never care for a home like its owner, but their mental and emotional issues will also manifest through the home. Because they are not responsible for the repairs, there is almost a reckless abandon with their emotions in a space. This of course is not the case with all renters as many people have an innate appreciation of their personal space. If you rent out your home, just know that not only are your tenants residing there physically, but emotionally as well. When you rent a home that you have lived in, your energy and that of your renters are both intertwined in the space. This is a different dynamic than homes purchased and rented for investment purposes.

Moving

Moving is one of the most stressful times in our life. When we move, it is a literal and energetic uprooting of our energy. It affects us on all levels - the physical, mental, emotional, and spiritual levels. Our home is our center, our grounding, and our sense of self. When we move, this all gets thrown up. For a few hours, days, or weeks, depending on the process, we are in transition and unclear of who we are. When we land in our new space, we start all over in getting acclimated to the energy of the new space. As we start to unpack and put our personal stamp on the space, we start to feel home again. We are home again amongst our books, pictures, and other belongings that hold our energy, memories, and emotions.

Moves always accompany major transitions in our life. If you think back to the times you have moved, it most likely coincided with a major occurrence. They usually indicate an ending and a new beginning. We move because a job begins or ends, a baby is born or a child goes to college, starting a new school or graduation, the start of a relationship or the ending of one. We even refer back to periods of our life based on the house in which we lived at the time. A move marks a new chapter in our life. It allows us to start over and start anew. It is a time to evaluate what you want to change and do differently in your life as the new home will allow for a new beginning. It holds a new energy that will allow for new opportunities.

Prior to or upon moving into a new space it is important to recognize the home as its own unique soul. Approach the home as you would in getting to know anyone in a new relationship. It is advisable to space clear the home prior to, or soon thereafter, moving in. Have a ceremony or blessing for the home. If it feels appropriate, you can even name the home thereby honoring its energy. In doing so, you will also be honoring yourself and your time while living there. Recognize the significance of the home in your life and how it can support you with where you are in the current phase of your journey.

Just as important as honoring your new home is honoring the home from which you moved. For some spaces, we can't get out fast enough. Perhaps it holds bad memories and emotions or represents a phase in life that we would rather forget about. On the other hand, there are those spaces that are so difficult to move from. They hold special memories and it feels painful to remove ourselves from the space as if we are one with it. In either case, however, it is imperative to have closure with the space. There is no right or wrong way to do this and should be done intuitively. The overall goal is to say *Thank You* to the space thereby honoring your time while living there and also taking your energy from the space. In doing so, you will have emotional closure over your time while living there as well.

Each time I move from a space, I have some time alone with the home. After the moving trucks have left, I go to each room. I think back on all the memories - the good and the bad - and let them wash through me. I then say *Thank You* to each room and to the house as a whole. On an energetic level, we are taking back parts of our energy that would otherwise remain in the home. By having closure with the home, it helps space clear the space for future owners as well. It is when we deny or try to stuff our emotions that they continue to haunt us (and the home) in some way. Or the same emotions and patterns follow us to our next space. Honoring the previous home will allow for a brighter new beginning going into the next home. If you have not done this with prior spaces, it's possible to do this retroactively through a meditation download on my website, called *Soul Retrieval Through Space*.

Conclusion

Mahatma Ghandi stated, "Our contribution to the progress of the world must consist in setting our own house in order." Regardless of whether he was referring to our "house" literally or figuratively, the message is that we each have personal responsibility for taking care of our individual lives represented through our living spaces.

If we each put our own home in order - whether it is using feng shui principles to bring about peace and harmony or decorating our home to where we love coming home - we are bettering our lives and the Planet. If we each take care of the plot of space we take up on the Earth, it will be an even more beautiful world in which to live. This of course carries over to businesses and municipality spaces as well. But the change has to start in our personal spaces and how we treat and love ourselves. This is consistent with Ghandi's more famous quote, "Be the change you want to see in the world."

Our spaces are so important to our overall health and wellbeing and have been vastly overlooked in their importance. Restaurants and retailers know that the vibe and feel of the space can make or break its businesses. Design, feng shui, and the overall feel of a space have become paramount in our economy - from the sleek design of technology products to the real estate market. Corporations are also realizing the importance of space with regards to employee retention. Forward-thinking companies, such as Google, Facebook, and Apple incorporate community spaces, lounges, and other nontraditional office environments within the office.

Hospitals and health-care facilities are also starting to understand the need for better design and how it affects the health of the patients. Even universities and sports teams use space as a recruitment tool by pouring millions into a high-end facility to coax players. Studies in environmental psychology are showing the positive effects of space on productivity and overall happiness in our workday. The same is true when we come home to a space we love to be in. It is my hope that everyone has access to information or resources to bring about peace, love, and harmony into their living and work spaces.

REFERENCE OF MIND BODY HOME CONNECTIONS

	Symbolism or Meaning	Mental/Emotional/Physical Association
Air Filter	Filtering toxins from your life	Breathing issues particularly pertaining to inhaling. What are you taking in that is not in your highest and best interest?
Ants	Annoyances in day-to-day life Industry; productivity, efficiency Distractions	Underutilizing or misdirecting your energy. Re-examine day-to-day routines
Attic	Higher state of consciousness Connection to Higher Self Spirituality or Religion Inherited belief systems Old family patterns Goals and aspirations	Relates to the 7th Chakra Headaches Feeling disconnected Feeling lost, confused, or lonely
Balcony	Special and unique talent or skill	What skills or talents are you underutilizing or not taking advantage of?
Basement	Subconscious mind The past Old identities Repressed emotions	Relates to 2nd Chakra Small intestines Reproductive organs Excretory organs Feelings of guilt or regret Stagnation Holding on to the past Lack of trust
Bathroom	Self-care Releasing	See associations for individual components within the bathroom.

Bathtub	Self-care Nurturing oneself Cleansing	Detoxifying the body and/or emotions
Bedroom	Intimacy Relaxation Rejuvenation Tranquility Dreaming Partnership love or self-love	Taking time out for relationship with self or others Restoring personal energy
Bonus Room (or Recreation Room)	Recreation Fun Hobbies Children	Do you incorporate enough fun into your life?
Burglars	Allowing others to take your energy Violation of personal space	Where are you allowing yourself to be violated? Where are you giving away your energy? Where do you need a wake-up call in your life?
Ceiling	"Glass ceiling" "The sky's the limit" Perspective	Feeling expansive or constricted Ability to spread your wings
Closet	"Skeletons in the closet" "Coming out of the closet" What do you not want to look at? What are you hiding?	Fear of being yourself Authenticity Denying an aspect of yourself
Cockroaches	Survival Spiritual cleansing	Fear of the unknown Confusion Scattered
Clogged Pipe	Bottled up emotions Control	Inability to communicate emotions Unable to release emotions

Clogged Toilet	Unable to release emotions
Hanging on to toxic emotions	Constipation or diarrhea
Intestinal disorders
Tension or stress
Deck (or Patio)	Extension of energy	Where are you underutilizing yourself?
Den (also Living Room)	Our personality
Basic beliefs and values
Daily living routine
Family	Heart and lungs
Are you able to personally express yourself?
Dining Room	Nurturing
Warmth
Communal
Family	Digestion
Are you taking adequate care of yourself?
Door	Opportunities
Possibilities	Shoulders, hips, joints.
Being open-minded
Being seen
Doorbell	Messages
Being open to opportunities when they come	Being receptive
Being open-minded
Doorknob	Making connections
Having a "handle" on things	Hands
Misconnections
Over-controlling
Driveway	Transition between home and the world
Pathway between the known and unknown	How connected or disconnected are you from the rest of the world?
What is a safe distance from the world?
Electricity	Power
Life force
Energy level	Nervous system
High blood pressure
Overworked
Exhausted
Lethargy

Electrical wiring	How one channels energy	Short or quick tempered High strung Confused, scattered Attention deficit
Exterior material	Protection Outer protective layer	Skin-related disorders Being tough- or thin-skinned Feeling safe and protected
Fence	Boundaries Being "on the fence"	Not setting adequate boundaries Indecisiveness
Fireplace	Family Warmth Traditional values "Heart of the home"	Digestive fires Heart-related Escape of energy
Flies	Mental annoyances	Scattered Inability to focus
Flooding	Cleansing or clearing Detoxing energy that is no longer a vibrational match for you. Letting go.	Colons. Analogous to colonic hydrotherapy. Related to 2nd chakra clearing.
Flooring	Division between levels of consciousness Proper boundaries Grounded	Energy leaks Feeling tired, lethargy, overused and underappreciated. Not a clear sense of self
Floors or Stories	Levels of consciousness. Where the "stories" of our life take place.	See association for each individual floor
Foundation	Having a solid foundation in life Family issues Indecisiveness Ungrounded	Feet, knees, or legs problems Mental anxiety Blood-related disorders Immune system Issues relating to 1st Chakra Feeling flighty or scattered

Framework	Internal architecture	Bones Misalignment in skeleton Major shift in belief systems Unexpected trauma
Front Porch	How one portrays themselves to the world Welcoming Neighborly Putting your "best foot forward"	Chin Face Foot
Frozen pipes	Emotionally frozen	Poor blood circulation
Garden	Abundance Growth Expansion	Money Happiness Joy Gratefulness
Garage	Utilitarian Functional Mechanical	Clutter Stagnant Overwhelmed Inefficient
Ghosts	Allowing others to take up your space Not fully owning your space	Underutilizing oneself Not feeling good enough Feeling a lack of something in your life
Hallways	Veins and arteries of the home Connectors Transition spaces	Breathing Short of breath Feeling overwhelmed "Walls coming in"
Heating & Air System (HVAC)	Breath of the home	Respiratory system Breathing Exhaustion Overworked
Hot Water Heater	Emotions with fire power	Emotions bubbling up to the surface most likely in the form of anger

Insects	Annoyances What is "bugging" you?	See associations for specific insects.
Internet	Connection Communication	Inability to connect of communicate with the world Feeling aloof Needing alone time
Kitchen	Nurturing center of the home "Heart of the home"	Related to the heart and breasts Feeling the need to nurture oneself or family
Key lock	Information Answers	Not wanting to come home Anxiety Misunderstanding
Light Switch	How you control your energy or power. Yin and yang	Being "on" or "off"
Living Room (or Den)	Our personality Basic beliefs and values Daily living routine Family	Heart and lungs Are you able to personally express yourself?
Main Level or Floor	Present consciousness Reflection of daily life Personal expression	Mental clarity Ability to focus or concentrate Obsessive-compulsive
Mouse	Holes in your life Energy leaks Taking power over your life Taking up space in the world	Where are others taking your power? Do you need to take a stand on something? Are you under-exerting your power in the world?
Patio (or Deck)	Extension of energy	Where are you underutilizing yourself?
Plumbing	Channeling of emotions	Colons Excretory organs

Recreation Room (or Bonus Room)	Recreation Fun Hobbies Children	Do you incorporate enough fun into your life?
Roof	Protection Connection with Source Spirituality	Headaches, migraines. Vulnerability Surrender Open to a higher power
Second Level or Floor	Higher states of consciousness Relaxation and tranquility Dreaming	Relates to 6th Chakra Intuition Dreams and visions Headaches Escapism
Shower	Self-care Cleansing Releasing	Releasing emotions Surrender
Stairs	Journey to a higher level of consciousness	Related to throat and neck Are you getting "tripped up" on your journey?
Stove	Power	Are you fully utilizing your personal power?
Swimming Pool	Abundance Flowing Renewal	Are you feeling drained?
Telephone	Communication with others	Difficulties pertaining to speaking Do you feel misunderstood or not heard?
Toilet	Release Surrender Letting go that which no longer serves you	Excretory system

Toilet Seat	Taking time to release emotions	Hurried Not taking time for self-care
Toilet Flusher	A final release	Hesitancy in releasing emotions
Trees	Life Growth Abundance Balance Grounded	Cleansing Shift in belief system Shift in foundational support
Walls	Limitations, obstacles, or boundaries Open-minded vs. closed-minded	Neck and throat issues. Respiratory and blood flow Having tunnel vision Feeling blocked creatively
Windows	New perspectives Seeing the big picture Seeing outside of yourself Open to other's opinions and viewpoints	Eyes Vision Clairvoyance Refusing to see what's in front of you Lack of clarity

BIBLIOGRAPHY

Day, Christopher, *Places of the Soul* (The Aquarian Press, 1990)

Skinner, *Sacred Geometry: Deciphering the Code* (Sterling 2009)

Hay, Louise, *You Can Heal Your Life* (Hay House 2009)

Chopra, Deepak, *The Book of Secrets* (Harmony Books 2004).

Bachelard, Gaston, *The Poetics of Space* (Beacon Press 1994)

Alexander, Christopher, *The Timeless Way of Building* (Oxford University Press 1979)

Alexander, Christopher, *A Pattern Language* (Oxford University Press 1977)

Assaraf, John and Smith, Murray, *The Answer* (Atria Books 2009)

Andrews, Ted *Animal-Speak* (Llewellyn Publications 1995)

Linn, Denise, *Sacred Space* (Wellspring/Ballantine 1995)

Jung, C.G., *Memories, Dreams, Reflections* (Vintage 1989)

Marcus, Clare Cooper, *House as a Mirror of Self* (Nicolas-Hays 2006)

ABOUT THE AUTHOR

Tisha Morris is a feng shui expert, attorney, and self-help author who has been featured on *Live with Kelly and Ryan, Hay House Radio, Today.com, Elle Decor, ABC News,* and *Well + Good.*

Tisha has a degree in law, economics, and interior design with certifications in yoga, feng shui, and coaching. Tisha advises and represents clients using her entrepreneurial experience, legal and publishing expertise, intuition, and practical wisdom to help clients realize their potentials, clear blocks, and strategize for optimal success.

When not working with clients, Tisha lives in Ojai, California, with her wife, poodle, two stepcats, and works on becoming a legal thriller novelist. For more information, visit www.tishamorris.com.

www.ingramcontent.com/pod-product-compliance
Lightning Source LLC
Chambersburg PA
CBHW031106080526
44587CB00011B/845